338.4
LAN

At Issue

What Is the Future of the Music Industry?

Other Books in the At Issue Series:

At Issue

What Is the Future of the Music Industry?

Ronald D. Lankford, Jr., Book Editor

GREENHAVEN PRESS
A part of Gale, Cengage Learning

Detroit • New York • San Francisco • New Haven, Conn • Waterville, Maine • London

Elizabeth Des Chenes, *Director, Publishing Solutions*

© 2013 Greenhaven Press, a part of Gale, Cengage Learning

Gale and Greenhaven Press are registered trademarks used herein under license.

For more information, contact:
Greenhaven Press
27500 Drake Rd.
Farmington Hills, MI 48331-3535
Or you can visit our Internet site at gale.cengage.com

For product information and technology assistance, contact us at

Gale Customer Support, 1-800-877-4253
For permission to use material from this text or product, submit all requests online at
www.cengage.com/permissions

Further permissions questions can be emailed to permissionrequest@cengage.com

Articles in Greenhaven Press anthologies are often edited for length to meet page requirements. In addition, original titles of these works are changed to clearly present the main thesis and to explicitly indicate the author's opinion. Every effort is made to ensure that Greenhaven Press accurately reflects the original intent of the authors. Every effort has been made to trace the owners of copyrighted material.

Cover photograph reproduced by permission of Brand X Pictures.

LIBRARY OF CONGRESS CATALOGING-IN-PUBLICATION DATA

What is the future of the music industry? (2013) What is the future of the music industry? / Ronald D. Lankford, Jr., book editor.
    p. cm. -- (At issue)
    Includes bibliographical references and index.
    978-0-7377-6211-2 (hardcover) -- ISBN 978-0-7377-6212-9 (pbk.)
    1. Sound recording industry. I. Lankford, Ronald D., 1962- II. Title.
    ML3790.W49 2013
    338.47'78--dc23

                                                        2012042877

Printed in the United States of America
1 2 3 4 5 6 7 17 16 15 14 13

Contents

Introduction

It was a before and after moment in the music industry. In October of 2007, the alternative band Radiohead decided to distribute *In Rainbows* as an online download. The band allowed fans to pay whatever they wanted for the music (including paying nothing at all). The "pay what you want to pay" download completely bypassed the middleperson—the record company—and 1.2 million copies of *In Rainbows* were downloaded on the first day of the album's release. With the success of Radiohead's independent release, the music industry would never be the same. "Clearly," one writer noted, "self-releasing *In Rainbows* was a smart business move on Radiohead's part."[1]

Traditionally, new bands had worked hard to gain the notice of the music industry. Typically, a band would play live gigs, gather an audience, and perhaps record a demo to send to record labels. If the band gathered a large following or caught the attention of an A&R (artists and repertoire) representative, it might receive a recording contract from a major record company, like Sony or Def Jam. Often, the record label would deduct the cost of the recording from the future earnings of the new band, which would have to be earned back by touring. Record labels, meanwhile, would help promote the new band with radio DJs and television personalities.

In essence, the music industry often controlled the band, unless the band was lucky enough to become very popular. The industry decided who would get recorded and, perhaps more importantly, who would not get recorded. And even when a band was chosen, it might only be given two years to become successful. If the initial trial was unsuccessful, then the band was simply dropped from the label.

Even for lesser-known bands, Radiohead's online strategy marked a seismic shift within the music industry: bands could bypass traditional methods of recording and distributing music. With computer technology and the Internet, most anyone could record and distribute music without record labels, radio stations, and record stores. "I like the people at our record company, but the time is at hand when you have to ask why anyone needs one," said Thom Yorke of Radiohead. "And, yes, it probably would give us some perverse pleasure to say 'F--- you' to this decaying business model."[2] Online, the band had direct access to its audience; online, the audience had direct access to the band. Whatever the size of the band, it was no longer necessary to follow the old rules.

While this old system continues at major recording labels, many other bands have followed in the path of Radiohead. "Because of the small profit percentage with major labels," one writer noted, "it makes more sense for artists today to either go with an indie label or self-release an album in order to actually turn a profit."[3] In 2005, a much lesser known band, Clap Your Hands Say Yeah, self-released its first album, eventually selling two hundred thousand copies. Soon, record labels were attempting to sign the band. The group, however, liked being independent: "The question that we asked record companies was essentially, 'What can you do for us that we can't do for ourselves?'"[4]

At first, Clap Your Hands Say Yeah pressed two thousand copies, then five thousand copies, and next ten thousand of its first album. As the band began to sell more copies and tour, it attracted more attention, including coverage from the influential music website, Pitchfork. As momentum for the band gathered, however, Clap Your Hands Say Yeah remained committed to staying independent.

"We've been talking to folks here and there about signing on," noted band member Alec Ounsworth, "but I like the idea of it being an independent operation as long as we can do it. But the fact of the matter is, there are five of us. We all have our own obligations, and it's very difficult between five of us to handle everything. So that would be the purpose of a label."[5]

Asked if he had advice for other bands trying to succeed, Ounsworth said:

> "Cross your fingers? No, just kidding. Nowadays, there are so many bands that are getting some sort of exposure [with the Internet] that there needs to be something about the band that stands out. I was talking to a friend who also has a band, and we remarked that we are at the point where we can see now that it's pretty clear that you don't go into music because you want to be famous and to make lots of money. So I think if you just keep on doing what you are doing, with a bit of luck, it's bound to happen."[6]

The new DIY (do-it-yourself) ethic has changed another aspect of the music industry. Once, choosing to work with a smaller label or go without a record label was defined as independent. Often, these bands were less concerned with commercial popularity and more focused on artistic integrity. Now, however, any band choosing to promote its career without a record label—even a band that becomes massively popular—can be defined as independent.

While working without a record label seems like a win-win situation for new bands, many questions remain in the quickly evolving music field. Radiohead, for instance, was already widely known before releasing an album independently. Record labels are also able to help with quality control and financial backing, ensuring a professional recording, well-made music videos, and the ability to tour broadly. By providing experience and bankrolling a band, then, a record label provides a safety net.

But many bands are no longer willing to wait to be discovered. And as in the case of Clap Your Hands Say Yeah, it may—for many aspiring musicians—no longer seem necessary. Clap Your Hands Say Yeah, after all, was not well known like Radiohead when it chose to independently release its first and second albums. Through hard work and talent, however, the band achieved popularity. While no one can predict exactly what the future of the music industry will look like, bands like Radiohead and Clap Your Hands Say Yeah have practically shut the door on the older model.

Notes

1. "From Disc to Digital: A Case Study on Radiohead's 'Name Your Own Price' Method," *Hub Pages*. http://rb101182 .hubpages.com/hub/From-Disc-to-Digital-Music-Industry-Business-Practices-in-the-21st-Century (accessed August 22, 2012).
2. Ibid.
3. Ibid.
4. David Morgan, "Real Band, No Record Company," *CBS Evening News*, February 11, 2009. http://www.cbsnews.com/ 2100-18563_162-2858961.html.
5. Monte Holman, "Clap Your Hands Say Yeah," *Free Williamsburg*, July 15, 2005. http://www.freewilliamsburg.com/clap -your-hands-say-yeah.
6. "Interview with Clap Your Hands Say Yeah," *Cape Town Magazine*. http://www.capetownmagazine.com/live-music/ Interview-with-Clap-Your-Hands-Say-Yeah/141_22_18581 (accessed August 22, 2012).

1

The Future of Music Technology: A History and Overview

Somin Lee

Somin Lee is a writer and layout editor for Yale Scientific Magazine.

Since the advent of MP3s, commentators have noted the quick pace of change within the music industry. The music industry, however, has always been subject to changes in technology. From cylinders, to vinyl, to cassettes, to compact discs, and to MP3s, the industry has undergone a series of small revolutions in how music is delivered to the consumer. Even today, new technology promises to one day make the iPod seem as old fashioned as the vinyl record.

The ubiquitous iPod is currently one of the most popular devices for listening to music, but it was not simply developed overnight. From the early cassettes to the compact disc, music technology has undergone drastic changes over the past century and will only continue to develop in the future.

In 1877, Thomas Edison introduced the phonograph, a device that consisted of a cylinder covered in tin foil, which was conducive to detecting small vibrations of a stylus as it cut groves into the cylinder in accordance with sound waves. This cylinder could then be removed, transferred to another phonograph, and the originally recorded sound could thus be reconstructed by using the vibrations recorded in the grooves. Alexander Graham Bell later modified Edison's phonograph by replacing the tin foil with wax, resulting in enhanced sound quality.

Ten years later, Emile Berliner invented the gramophone, which used a flat, zinc disc in lieu of a cylinder. Discs remained a popular medium to record and listen to music through the 1900s. Then, vinyl was introduced during World War II for sending discs to soldiers and continued to be the most popular medium for disc manufacturing even after the war.

With so many advancements looming on the horizon, we are sure to look back on our iPods with the same nostalgia that we now have for records and cassettes.

From Cassette Tapes to MP3s

The use of cassette tapes truly brought the music industry into the electronic age. However, although magnetic recording had been available since the 1930s, it did not become popular in the music industry until the mid 1960s. Early cassettes consisted of long rolls of tape covered with ferric oxide in a plastic shell. A small electromagnet within the cassette received audio input through a thin wire wrapped around the base of the magnet. This magnet created a flux that matched the audio input, so when a tape was pressed against the magnet, the metal particles recorded this information by permanently aligning themselves in accordance with the flux. Small and compact, cassettes also lead to Sony's development of the Walkman in 1979, introducing the first instance of portable music technology.

The 1970s also ushered in the beginning of the optical compact disc, or what we colloquially refer to as CDs. Composed of a polycarbonate plastic, CDs consist of millions of microscopic bumps arranged in a single spiral groove. Audio information is stored digitally in these grooves, similar to the small vibrations in record grooves. In order to read these bumps, a laser is shined on to the disc surface, and the slight disturbances in the reflection are detected and the digital signal is processed into sound.

Soon, developments in Internet technology and the introduction of the MPEG-1 Audio Layer 3, or MP3, format transformed the music industry. MP3 technology allows music files to be compressed up to 1/12 of their original sizes, facilitating the simple sharing of music on the Internet. Although Audio Highway created the first publicly available MP3 player in 1997, MP3 players did not become widely popular until the introduction of the iPod by Apple in 2001. The first iPod boasted a sleek, slender body and a memory capacity that could hold up to 1,000 songs. Its small size was achieved by using a microcontroller—a small computer originally designed for running automated machines, such as power tools and car engines. Microcontrollers are significantly smaller than the microprocessors that were found in previous MP3 players, allowing iPods to be much more compact.

The Future of Music

Music technology continues to evolve today and presents many exciting possibilities for the future. For example, potential future concepts for Apple products include technology that eliminates headphones by utilizing ultrasound technology and employing music players that will automatically sync to iTunes and charge via the Internet. In addition, these iPods are projected to have memory capacities that may reach the order of terabytes in the near future.

However, memory capacities may soon be meaningless with the introduction of online music streaming. Music is quickly merging with the computer revolution, and music sites, such as Spotify, allow users to stream millions of songs online for free. These websites combined with faster network speeds on mobile phones may soon provide music lovers with the entire Internet at their disposal. These technologies are only an inkling of what music technology might hold for the future. With so many advancements looming on the horizon, we are sure to look back on our iPods with the same nostalgia that we now have for records and cassettes.

2

Cloud-Based Music Services Are Changing the Way Music Is Accessed

Songtrust

Songtrust is a music start-up company that helps songwriters, artists, managers, labels, and publishers manage their music rights, including the administration of music publishing assets, performing rights, and digital licensing.

Cloud-based music is a new service that will allow consumers to store their music collections online. Amazon.com, for instance, has offered one of the first cloud-based services. Instead of transferring MP3s from one computer or device to another, cloud-based services allow users to access their music collection from any computer or phone with an Internet connection. While there have been legal challenges from song publishers, cloud-based music services seem likely to provide a new face for the future of the music industry.

For many of us in the music industry, 'cloud-based music services' have been an interesting topic of conversation for the past several months. There is an astounding level of curiosity and buzz for not only tech-savvy, music users across the world, but also labels, publishers, artists and songwriters. But what exactly do cloud services mean for the music industry? At this point, it really is too early to tell—but what we do know is that 'cloud music' has arrived.

"An Introduction to Cloud-Based Music Services," Songtrust.com, April 29, 2012. Copyright © 2012 by Songtrust. All rights reserved. Reproduced by permission.

The term, 'cloud-based music' is referring to a way of storing, managing and accessing your music collection through a digital storage space online. This storage space (often called a 'cloud' or 'music locker') would allow users to transfer their entire music collection to one secure site, which would be able to be accessed from anywhere at any time—all you would need is an internet connection.

Up until now, when you would purchase music (such as downloads), you could only play it on that device. Sure you could move your music, but this would require transferring the music by burning a cd, using a flash drive or sending large e-mail files of music. Cloud Music services, like the one Amazon.com has just launched, allow you to organize your entire library of music and access it as you wish. Whether you're walking around with your smart phone, sitting in front of your computer at work, at a friend's house on his laptop, etc.—you will be able to pull up your entire personal music collection, just by logging in.

Amazon's service will also allow its users to instantly send music that's been purchased from Amazon directly to their personal music cloud—while also allowing for manual uploads from iTunes libraries or other music sources. Currently, Amazon's Cloud Player allows up to 5GB of free storage (or roughly 1,000 songs) and gives you the option to upgrade the size of your cloud by purchasing storage plans, which start at around $20 per year. There are also a few perks that Amazon is throwing out there as well—all purchases made from Amazon will be stored free, and there is a promotion that allows 20 free GB for a year to any customer that downloads a full digital album from Amazon. There's also a rather lengthy 'Terms and Conditions' that you must agree to. . . .

Practical Applications

Now . . . logistics aside, let's apply this to the real world. I have a music library of about 8,000 songs on my personal computer at home and I have the luxury of working in an office where listening to music is highly encouraged, if not required. Anytime I would want to bring in music, I would either put it on a flash drive, or e-mail it to myself through file sharing sites like YouSendIt.com—which generally takes some time. For me, a cloud service appears to be the practical answer I'm looking for. To figure out just exactly how Amazon's Cloud Player works, I decided to take it for a test-run.

Being that this is such a new service, there are bound to be some bugs and glitches.

The first thing I needed to do was log in to my Amazon .com account (new users would be required to create a login/ password). At the top left of the Amazon homepage there is a link that reads MP3's & Cloud Player for Web. I followed the link and started creating my 'cloud.' Amazon's Cloud Player instantly began scanning my computer for music and notified me of the results.

After scanning my computer, I was informed that I had 7.9 GB (1,119 songs) available for upload (2.9 GB over the standard—and free—storage space). I was then prompted to either buy more storage space, edit what I wanted to upload or just upload everything that would fit. I decided to manually edit my selections and was re-directed to the 'Upload' page, where I was then able to pick and choose the specific music I wanted to upload, which would fit within the 5 GB storage space.

At this point I began uploading my songs to the cloud, which took some time (about 1.5 hours for 5 GB of music). When the upload was complete I was directed to my new personal 'Cloud Player' library. Here I found my collection of songs, all organized by artist, album, genre and song—available for either streaming or download. You can also create your own personal playlists in the cloud as well. When I got home from work, I immediately logged into Amazon to access my uploaded library from a different computer and there it was—ready for listening.

Cloud-Based Competition

What's going to be interesting is how both Apple and Google attempt to compete with Amazon, and how their cloud services will differ. Being that this is such a new service, there are bound to be some bugs and glitches—which have already plagued Amazon. This past week Amazon's Cloud Player experienced outages caused by connectivity and latency errors. The outages were corrected, but shined a light on how susceptible to errors these new services will be.

Despite the ongoing copyright and legal discussions, cloud music does appear to be in our immediate future.

While Amazon was the first in the race to launch a cloud-based music service, Apple and Google aren't that far behind. Just this month, Google registered dozens of 'cloud-related' domain names including GoogleThunder.com, GoogleLightning.com and GoogleNebula.com. Meanwhile, Apple has been inking licensing deals with major labels like Warner Music, in preparation of their cloud service launch. The Apple service is also widely rumored to have an initial free period, but will ultimately cost either a monthly or annual fee.

On the surface, it seems that Apple has been doing their homework by reaching agreements and terms with labels and publishers—something Amazon has yet to do. After facing legal threats, Amazon is now having to go back and strike up licensing deals with several music companies to avoid further scrutiny. Not surprisingly, there have been many legal challenges surrounding cloud-based music services. For starters, Amazon never consulted ASCAP [American Society of Composers, Authors and Publishers] or BMI [Broadcast Music,

Inc.], two performance rights organizations that see this service as a way to avoid paying songwriters, composers, artists and publishers for their content.

A similar music storage site, MP3Tunes.com, is currently being sued by 14 publishing companies and record labels for copyright infringement—mainly for allowing users to store unauthorized downloads. However, there "still hasn't been a square decision saying it's lawful to store copyrighted songs," says copyright attorney Jim Berger. "There is still some debate that it's not necessarily considered a fair use to share and make copies of content for personal use."

A Cloud-Based Future

Despite the ongoing copyright and legal discussions, cloud music does appear to be in our immediate future—and with the rise of these services are coming other complimentary companies.

Take for example, RealNetworks' Rinse—a new service dedicated to cleaning up the metadata in its customers music libraries. Rinse labels itself as a 'song organizer' that adds album artwork, corrects misspellings, deletes duplicates, renames genres, etc. As we all know, the major problem with our music libraries is that, for the most part, they are disorganized and messy. Some songs were burned from cd's, some were downloaded from P2P [peer-to-peer] sites, some were bought from iTunes, etc. As we're entering a world where all of our music can be stored and accessed from cloud service, the need to categorize existing libraries has a much higher importance than it previously did. The software can either fix entries automatically or allow its users to edit proposed changes. Rinse costs $40, works with both Mac and PC's and comes with a free trial for up to 50 tracks.

3

The Music Industry Has Been Revolutionized

Greg Kot, as interviewed by Kyle Bylin

Greg Kot is a music critic for The Chicago Tribune *and author of* Ripped: How the Wired Generation Revolutionized Music. *Kyle Bylin is an associate editor for Hypebot.com.*

In an interview with Kyle Bylin of Hypebot.com, author Greg Kot discusses the future of the music industry. The industry, Kot notes, has never been very adept at dealing with change. The status quo, if profitable, is seldom challenged. Unfortunately, this attitude has left the music industry unable to respond to the revolution of online music. With the old model of record labels, bands, and music distribution gradually disintegrating, fans and musicians have created many niche markets and communities on their own. As a result, the future of music is becoming more democratic, with the fans playing an important role in the development of the artist. Likewise, the music industry will have to respond to these developments, finding a balance between making music easily available and turning a profit.

Today, I spoke with Greg Kot, who is the author of *Ripped: How the Wired Generation Revolutionized Music*, a rock critic at *The Chicago Tribune*, and co-host of the popular radio show *Sound Opinions*. In this interview, Greg talks about the media landscape, the end of the mass-marketed mega artist, and adds his thoughts to 'the file-sharing debate.'

Kyle Bylin: Do you think we largely and often times do forget that for every action the Record Industry made in the media landscape there was an equal and opposite reaction from the general public, which only contributed to further evolving the complex system of relationships that had been created in the twentieth-century?

Greg Kot: I think there is a central motif here: The 20th Century record industry has never been particularly eager to embrace new technology, basically anything that threatened the status quo. It wasn't so much greed and arrogance that destroyed it as fear of change. They lost touch with consumers, and got comfortable riding a pricey cash cow—the compact disc.

But the system was inherently flawed; it worked for a long time because the industry basically seized monopoly control of manufacturing, distribution and marketing of music. Only the best-financed music stood a chance of getting heard, which usually meant bland releases by multimedia celebrities, whether Britney Spears or Creed. Consumers had no other choice put to play along, and pay what the industry demanded. When an alternative emerged, consumers naturally gravitated toward a market that allowed them greater access to more music at a better price.

The businessmen running these companies saw change as riskier than maintaining the status quo (and their jobs). They were wrong.

In his seminal release Stumbling on Happiness *Harvard Psychologist Dan Gilbert explains that, "When imagination paints a picture of the future, many of the details are necessarily missing, and imagination solves this problem by filling in the gaps with details that it borrows from the present."*

Throughout the vibrant history of the Record Industry how often have music executives tried to protect established cultural norms, position themselves financially and politically, and then failed, simply because they almost always err by predicting that the future would look too much like the present?

I'm not sure if it's a dearth of imagination so much as a reluctance to embrace change. When a business is successful and running relatively well, there is always a chance that any change in that system could result in a less successful financial result. As the stakes got higher, that mentality exerted a choke-hold on the industry. The industry was reluctant to make the jump from CDs/physical retail/terrestrial radio/MTV because it had built an extremely successful business on the back of those institutions.

By 1999 the music industry was the biggest revenue-earning entertainment industry in North America. So why change? Why embrace the Futureworld when the profits are rolling in, quarterly profit statements are fat, and stockholders are happy? The businessmen running these companies saw change as riskier than maintaining the status quo (and their jobs). They were wrong.

Within the Record Industry we've seen the continuous compression of the creativity timeline. First, due the abandonment of artist development once major labels became publically traded companies and focused on blockbuster albums. Second, due to the instantaneous nature of the Internet and how it amplifies word of mouth, the growth curve for an artist has compressed from a few years to a few weeks.

Has the continuous compression of the creativity timeline established unrealistic expectations for artists to adhere to and, in turn, does it paradoxically reduce the opportunity for most artists to ever develop to their "true potential?"

The career curve has accelerated. It's harder to keep a secret, to fly under the radar these days, and hence bands with potential and promise get elevated to next-big-thing status based on a YouTube video or a MySpace hit. It's an unavoidable side effect of viral word of mouth. A lot of bands aren't ready for that kind of attention so soon, but it's not the worst problem to have. The hard part is getting heard in the first place, and always will be. So patience is still key for any band, whether they get propped up too quickly by Internet buzz or not. Potential is only realized through perseverance, and that virtue will be tested in the instant-gratification culture we now live in.

The sale of recorded music is no longer the best way to measure an artist's success.

Within the domain of music why is it so hard to tell whether it's the culture of 'abundance' or 'scarcity' that's robbing average music fans of satisfaction?

Is there a satisfaction gap? Perhaps the consumer who depends on the big media companies to bring him music is dissatisfied by the dearth of choices. But the fan who is active in the niche music communities thriving on the Net is having a ball discovering, discussing and downloading new music. What's interesting to me is that the curated experience is so readily available for fans who want to find new music on the Web. Yes, this has created myriad little niches without a whole lot of economic clout as measured by the standards of the music biz. But, really, was the success rate much better in the past, when more than 90 percent of new releases by the major labels were considered failures because they didn't sell enough to recoup their budgets?

To my mind, the sale of recorded music is no longer the best way to measure an artist's success. Look at Girl Talk and Dan Deacon, two artists I discuss in the book—if you measured their cultural standing by record sales, they would be completely obscure. But that's obviously not the case. The notion of building a community around an artist is more viable than ever, and it may have nothing to do with traditional economic measurements like Soundscan, chart position or radio airplay. . . .

Would you consider the mass-marketing successes that occurred during the CD-Boom a relatively short-lived phenomenon and, if so, why and what's some of your reasoning behind that belief?

Yes, I think the era of the mass-marketed mega artist is coming to an end. The multimedia companies that once dominated the star-maker discourse no longer monopolize how music is accessed. The culture for entertainment, as well as everything else for that matter, is fragmenting into niches facilitated by tools that enable us to find and communicate with people who have similar interests more efficiently and quickly than ever.

I do think the multimedia celebrities like Madonna, J-Lo, U2 will still exist in the domain of the multinational conglomerates, which are well-equipped to market and exploit such celebrities. They're brilliant at selling product across multiple platforms on a large scale. But for the vast majority of artists, the notion of the big major-label deal will be an absurd artifact of the late 20th Century. It has no relevance to what they do or how they communicate with their audience. An artist won't need to sign with a major to make a living, and the art will get a lot more interesting as a result.

The notion of being able to download any song at any time anywhere is soon going to be a reality and it will pretty much change the game irrevocably.

In Did You Know, *it says that "NTT Japan has successfully tested a fiber optic cable . . . that pushed 14 trillion bits per second down a single stand of fiber. That is 2,660 CDs every second." Couple that with Digital Renaissance's Martin J. Thörnkvist who writes, "In five years a hard drive available to ordinary consumers will carry 35 TB of data. Data = music. 35 TB = 2.5 million songs."*

What implications do you think these technological advances may have on 'the file-sharing debate' and, will the Record Industry ever be prepared for the trajectory of where things seem to be heading?

The notion of being able to download any song at any time anywhere is soon going to be a reality and it will pretty much change the game irrevocably. Artists and copyright holders will have to relinquish control of their work as soon as it's released. So will recorded music be free? Not necessarily. What if Steve Jobs had to share profits from the iPod with copyright holders? Similarly, the developers of the portable systems designed to access music in the future will/should share the wealth for the music/movies/media content they access.

Just because artists give up control of their art doesn't mean they should relinquish being compensated for it. The price has to be fair. In return fans should be able to get any music they want whenever they want, with top quality sound. It could be a win-win for artists and fans, and a new industry could develop around that relationship to facilitate it through instant, high-quality downloads, with some sort of service fee imposed on the hardware/software used to access the music.

Consumers are no longer just a marketing demographic, a faceless entity to which corporations market and sell products. They're becoming collaborators, co-conspirators, creative partners with the artists they love.

Authors [John] Palfrey and [Urs] Gasser argue in Born Digital *that, "Digital Natives will move markets and transform industries, education, and global politics. The changes they bring about as they move into the workforce could have an immensely positive effect on the world we live in."*

In what ways do you think the 'Wired Generation' will continue to revolutionize music and do they have the potential to create culture in which we will all be operating in the future?

Absolutely. The fundamental change is this: Consumers are no longer just a marketing demographic, a faceless entity to which corporations market and sell products. They're becoming collaborators, co-conspirators, creative partners with the artists they love. That intimacy is the key to remaking the world. All great artists over time have had their benefactors and patrons. The Internet makes it possible for a creative talent to have more of them than ever, on a potentially global scale.

A Black Swan, as described by Nassim Nicholas Taleb, is a highly improbable event with three principal characteristics: It is unpredictable; it carries a massive impact; and, after the fact, we concoct an explanation that makes it appear less random, and more predictable, than it was.

Seeing as the Music Industry has succumbed to its fair share of Black Swans over the last decade, do you feel like the ten years hold the same fate?

I think the impact of the most recent Black Swan invasion will still be playing itself out in 10 years. The way music is being made, manufactured, marketed, distributed and consumed is already in the midst of a radical change. We're not sure how it's all going to play out, but we're heading there—fast. I bet the music industry as we now know it is going to be quite a bit different in 2019. . . .

The hubris of the 20th Century music industry never ceases to amaze me. It's just a grain of sand when set against the vast history of music.

It seems like, that when people talk about the architecture of the record industry, they do so in a manner that alludes to this idea that it's a natural system.

When, in fact, this system is not; it developed over the course of a century and was designed by certain people at a certain moment in history. It was built from the ground up—at the expense of other social mechanisms and ecologies—and then, in the wake of the digital revolution, the record industry used its existence as evidence that this is the way things have always been.

Has this kind of thinking prevented us, mostly the record industry, from recognizing the true potential of music culture online, and caused them to think of music as something that overlays on top of the web, rather than as something that's vital to the social fabric of it?

The hubris of the 20th Century music industry never ceases to amaze me. It's just a grain of sand when set against the vast history of music.

The Internet, above all, is a tool for sending and receiving files. That music files would be part of that culture is only natural.

I mean, music played a vital social, cultural and political role long before recorded music was possible, and it continues to play a vital role now that the business model that developed around recorded music has started to crumble. More people are listening to more music than at any time in history, which as a premise for a business can't be bad. But it demands a different business model than the one that dominated as recently as a decade ago, which was essentially a very narrow pipeline that filtered a select group of music from a select group of anointed artists to the vast majority of consumers.

The music industry was used to being a monopoly, the primary arbiter and distributor of recorded music, and now it's competing with millions of arbiters and distributors—listeners with cell phones and laptops. That strikes me as a far more natural and organic system than the corporate model that emerged in the last half of the 20th Century. The shelf life of that model was destined to be a short one, since it was so restrictive.

Something that's always interested me about the file-sharing debates is what I call the anti-corporate argument. As Nate Harden said a few months back, "My generation's attitude toward piracy is not likely to change. After all, anti-corporate rebellion is a time-honored Rock 'n' Roll tradition. It's relatively easy to steal music if you imagine that you are merely stealing from 'The Man'—some limo-riding fat cat, snorting coke off his Rolex, sipping Dom Pérignon."

I've never really thought of file-sharing as anti-corporate rebellion, but as the pure embodiment of consumerism and our credit culture. In that, much like a credit card, file-sharing encourages fans to consume more music than they could ever afford, without ever challenging them to think twice about whether or not they will ever be able to pay artists back for the songs that are now in their possession.

Do you think this idea of "anti-corporate rebellion" is over-exaggerated, and that file-sharing, as a social behavior, is far more complex than that? So too, do you think that it's more consumerist than anti-corporate?

There's an element of the file-sharing community that's in stick-it-to-the-man outlaw mode, but I'm convinced the majority just get off on the convenience, the instant access. One quote from a file-sharer I interviewed sums it up: "It doesn't feel wrong." You're talking about a non-violent activity largely in the privacy of your own home, or bedroom or dorm room, in search of great music that turns you on—that is inherently a joyful, if potentially addictive, activity. It's also completely organic: The Internet, above all, is a tool for sending and receiving files. That music files would be part of that culture is only natural.

In Ripped, *you wrote. "For decades, popular music has been the art form most attuned and best equipped to offer instant feedback on the world outside the concert hall and the recording studio. In any given year, music offered more than an escapist release. It presented a running commentary on who we are and where we are as a society."*

During the last few years, we have arguably encountered some of the most multifaceted and complex problems we've ever faced. Do you think music served as an instrument to interpret these times to audiences, or has it served more as an escapist release?

Both. There's plenty of escapism out there, but there's also commentary and substance. I'm thinking of recent albums by Gorillaz, Ted Leo, Shearwater, the Fall and Dessa, that try to make sense of the world around us. It's an anxious, uncertain time, and this music reflects it. And then there's the Black Eyed Peas and American Idol for those who just want to switch off their brains and roll with it.

Commercial radio plays a very narrow sliver of music and it presents a very distorted picture of the creativity that actually exists.

In Empire of Illusion, *Chris Hedges argues that, "The worse reality becomes, the less a beleaguered population wants to hear about it, and the more it distracts itself with the squalid pseudo-events of celebrity breakdowns, gossip, and trivia."*

Has our popular music culture, due in part to the evolution of commercial radio and the economic woes of the record industry, become pressured, in a sense, to where there is less incentive for artists to raise important questions and interpret this complexity? Or is it also that the audience, judging by the charts, doesn't want to hear about it anymore?

It has always been so. I don't think this time is any more or less vacuous than any other in terms of the kind of art being created. Commercial radio plays a very narrow sliver of music and it presents a very distorted picture of the creativity that actually exists. I mean, more than 115,000 albums/CDs/pieces of recorded music were released last year—that's a lot of art/creativity that the world isn't hearing through mass media.

The Internet revealed the lie that commercial radio has become. The charts are less representative of what most people are actually listening to than ever before. There is music that is raising questions and engaging with the culture on a more complex level, it's just not fodder for corporate radio stations interested in selling advertising to their listeners. . . .

A lot of license holders and corporate interests are still mired in 20th Century business models, and that has made the transition much slower and more difficult than it should be.

Cultural critic Douglas Rushkoff has made the point that, "What [people are] missing from a cultural perspective is just because we're not willing to pay for professional journalists doesn't mean that corporations have become unwilling to pay for professional public relations departments."

He continues, "So we have governments and corporations and lobbies hiring the most expressive people they can to obfuscate reality, and the people being increasing unwilling pay for professionals to deconstruct that obfuscation, to ask the follow up question that makes their illusion drop like a house of cards."

Do we underestimate the role of the artist, writer, and journalist?

How does the saying go, "You don't know what you got till it's gone"? Creative people—and I include journalists—all play a vital role in keeping a culture vibrant, and will continue to do so even as trafficking in intellectual property becomes a lot dicier as a means of making a living.

People who create are driven to do it, and economics plays only a small role in why they continue to do what they do. As long as we have people creating, we will always have a running commentary. It's just that the means of accessing it and distributing it will change.

Knowing now—that you helped the general public better understand the plight of the record industry in the digital age— does that ennoble you to a certain degree? Is there anything particular that you wished you had more time to deconstruct and sort through the confusion, and to help people understand the issue better?

I'm privileged to be a reporter at a time when the world is changing irrevocably. With the onset of the Music Industry 2.0, and by extension the reinvention of all intellectual property, we're living through a historic time. The last 10 years were a pretty heady time to be alive, a time when a door was opened to a new way of creating and distributing music, a period worth documenting in a book. If there's a frustration, it's that I'm convinced the next 10 years will be even more exciting in terms of the possibilities that are opened up. Sequel?

Instead of trying to leverage free and artificial scarcity as mechanisms to combat this age of radical abundance, what do you think it will take for us to actually get past these means and learn how to start exchanging real value again—between people?

We'll get there. I think what's holding us back is that a lot of license holders and corporate interests are still mired in 20th Century business models, and that has made the transition much slower and more difficult than it should be. But the promise of Music 2.0 is that the relationship between artists and fans will be broader and deeper than ever before.

For me the central point of the story chronicled in *Ripped* is that the relationship has already moved in that direction, irrevocably. Listeners are no longer a demographic, they're patrons and tastemakers who now collaborate and conspire with artists. Our courts and government are slow to adapt to this rapid change, because these institutions tend to be very deliberate, but as the under-25 generations move into power, watch out.

4

Digital Music Platforms Are Transforming Publishing Industries

Scott Berinato

Scott Berinato maintains a blog at Harvard Business Review.

Research at the Harvard Business Review *has suggested an "iTunes effect" in the music industry. Because many consumers now purchase single tracks instead of albums, profits on album sales have decreased dramatically. This effect makes it increasingly difficult for record labels to make money from new bands; likewise, it is difficult for new bands to make a profit. Unless the music industry alters its practices, it will probably be unable to survive the digital revolution.*

How appropriate that this inaugural post in the Research blog focuses on the deleterious effect digital platforms are having on publishing. Seems as good a place to start as any, and Harvard Business School Associate Professor Anita Elberse . . . is doing some excellent research on the topic.

Her latest paper . . . is an excellent analysis of what might be called "the iTunes effect" and it tracks what happens to music sales as more people adopt digital purchasing of music. It's as bad as you'd expect, and probably worse.

Elberse studied music sales for more than 200 artists over more than two years. She found that people are buying more music than they used to, but because more are buying online, they're buying singles instead of full albums. The revenue from all those extra songs they buy doesn't come close to making up for the revenue lost on the albums they don't buy.

Decreased Album Sales

How bad is it? Elberse estimates that during her study, for every one-percent increase in users who move to online buying of music, there's a six-percent decrease in album sales. Average weekly sales for a "mixed bundle" (an album and its singles sold through all channels) dropped from $15,000 in early 2005 to about $7,000 in early 2007. Ouch. Despite selling lots of songs, record companies are making less than half as much on an album and its songs, because more people have the option to choose the single rather than buying the album to get the single. Elberse also found out that adding songs to a bundle but charging the same price (which theoretically should make more people buy the whole album because of increase perceived value) did not increase album sales. The only marginally good news that Elberse reports is that recent price increases on iTunes don't seem to have deterred buying.

Significantly decreased revenues breaks the cycle that helps find new talent that will generate more revenue.

Though it hasn't been studied across other kinds of content, it's conceivable that similarly impossible economics are playing out with any content that's getting unbundled and distributed digitally the way music is, such as stories like this one which, not that long ago, you'd need to buy a whole magazine or newspaper to get access to.

Elberse points out that the marketing literature usually focuses on the benefits of "mixed bundling"—offering a product and its components in different configurations to satisfy different consumer needs. But it's killing content publishing industries, which so far have no good answers to make up for the lost revenue.

But so what, right? Consumers are getting what they want. Why should I have to buy the album "I am . . . Sasha Fierce" . . . if all I want is the song "Single Ladies (Put a Ring on It)?" . . .

The Need for Industry Change

It's not that simple. Not all of that lost revenue was profit. That album revenue was partly subsidizing the discovery and publishing of new music, which in turn created new buyers of music, tour tickets, posters, t-shirts, and so on. That revenue in turn helped develop that artist's next venture, and discover yet other artists. Significantly decreased revenues breaks the cycle that helps find new talent that will generate more revenue.

Elberse discovered that the acts most protected from (though not completely protected from) the precipitous decline in album sales are, in fact, established acts. People still buy U2's albums, for example, at a higher rate than "creative workers without a strong reputation." This played out in my life recently. I bought U2's "No Line on the Horizon;" . . . without thinking twice, but when that new song . . . by the Avett Brothers caught my ear, not knowing the band as well, I just wanted to download that song. And I easily could. Can the Avett Brothers, in today's music economy, build their careers on sales of singles? Could U2 have become U2 if they built their careers starting now?

Probably not. The industry must change or die. Perhaps the concept of an album, of 11 songs by an artist, will become obsolete. Perhaps artists will have to "sell out" to video games and placement in advertisements and TV shows (as many have done) with increasing frequency. It's hard to know what's in store for music artists. Elberse's work shows the scope of the problem facing content producers today and the level of business re-invention necessary to support creative industries. So does this blog entry. After all, you didn't pay to read it, did you?

5

Music Piracy Is Obsolete

Economist

The Economist *is a British magazine that covers world economic, business, and cultural news.*

While commentators continue to debate the ethics of online file sharing, the age of piracy is over. Primarily, it is over because the complaints registered by consumers—about the quality and availability of online music—have been resolved. Instead of pursuing penalties for illegal file sharing, the music industry has worked to satisfy consumer demand. As a result, there is simply no longer a need to download music for free.

You open a window on your computer's screen. You type in the name of a cheesy song from the 1980s. A list of results appears. You double-click on one of them, and within a few seconds the song is playing. This is what it was like to use Napster a decade ago; and it is also how Spotify, another free online-music service, works today. The difference? Napster was an illegal file-sharing service that was shut down by the courts. Spotify, by contrast, is an entirely legal, free service supported by advertising. This shows how much things have changed in the world of online music in the past decade. It also explains why online music piracy may at last be in decline.

For most of the past decade the music industry focused on litigation to try to prevent piracy. Over the years the Recording Industry Association of America (RIAA) has accused

18,000 internet users of engaging in illegal file-sharing. Most of them settled, though two cases went to court this year. In both cases the defendants (a single mother and a student) lost and were ordered to pay damages (of $1.92m and $675,000 respectively). But the industry has realised that such cases encourage the publication of embarrassing headlines more than they discourage piracy, for as each network was shut down, another would sprout in its place.

There is growing evidence that this plethora of new services adds up to an attractive alternative to piracy for many.

Legal Alternatives

Yet as piracy flourished on illegal networks, legal alternatives also started to appear. Apple launched its iTunes Music Store, offering downloads at $0.99 per track, in 2003. Many others have followed, including a new, above-board version of Napster. And in the past two years new music sites and services have proliferated. Spotify offers free, advertising-supported streams; paying customers are spared the ads and can use the service on smart-phones. Nokia's Comes With Music scheme includes a year's unlimited downloads in the price of some mobile phones. TDC, a Danish telecoms operator, bundles access to a music service with its broadband packages.

All of these different, legal music services offer the "celestial jukebox"—whatever you want, right away, from the internet—that made Napster so compelling when it appeared on the scene. True, revenue from these services will be less than from CD sales, but it is much better than nothing. The recorded-music industry will get smaller—but it will not disappear.

That is because there is growing evidence that this plethora of new services adds up to an attractive alternative to piracy for many. . . . In June a poll of Swedish users of file-sharing software found that 60% had cut back or stopped using it; of those, half had switched to advertising-supported streaming services like Spotify. In Denmark, over 40% of subscribers to TDC's broadband-plus-music package also said they were making fewer illegal downloads as a result. In a British poll published in July, 17% of consumers said they used file-sharing services, down from 22% in December 2007. Music executives reckon people are moving from file-sharing networks to Spotify, though they may continue to download some music illegally.

Piracy thrives because it satisfies an unmet demand.

To be sure, the carrots of more attractive legal services are being accompanied by innovative forms of stick. In particular, a new approach called "graduated response" is gaining momentum. As its name indicates, it involves ratcheting up the pressure on users of file-sharing software by sending them warnings by e-mail and letter and then cutting off or throttling their internet access if they fail to respond after three requests. Graduated-response laws were introduced earlier this year in Taiwan and South Korea, and were enacted in France last month. Other countries are expected to follow suit.

Meeting Consumer Demand

Yet in Britain music file-sharing seems to be in decline even though a graduated-response law has yet to be introduced. The country also boasts one of the broadest selections of legal music services: Spotify and Comes With Music were both launched there before most other countries, and two of Britain's biggest internet-service providers have borrowed TDC's bundled-music model. This suggests that when it comes to discouraging music piracy, carrots may in fact be more important than sticks.

All of this offers a lesson for other types of media, such as films and video games. Piracy thrives because it satisfies an unmet demand. The best way to discourage it is to offer a diverse range of attractive, legal alternatives. The music industry has taken a decade to work this out, but it has now done so. Other industries should benefit from its experience—and follow its example.

6

Sharing Free Music Files Is Not Obsolete

Bruce Lidi

Bruce Lidi is a blogger who also works in public relations and community outreach.

The idea that the age of music piracy is over is wishful thinking. While iTunes and other online services may attract a following, most music fans continue to download free music. In order to survive, the music industry needs to understand this. While any easily reproducible file should remain free, music fans will continue to pay for tangible services such as concerts.

A provocative headline can generate a lot of readers and a lively debate, but it can also do a poor job of indicating what an article is actually about. A recent example is Paul Boutin's quite inflammatory article in the December edition of *Wired*, now available online, entitled rather ambitiously, "The Age of Music Piracy Is Officially Over." Based on the headline alone, a reader could assume that Boutin was making an interesting but factually incorrect observation about the state of file-trading online today. A quick glance at the comment section on the *Wired* site would indicate many people took exactly that viewpoint to blast Boutin.

However, that is not at all what the article actually argues. According to Boutin, we all need to "Mark down the date: The age of stealing music via the Internet is officially over. It's time for everybody to go legit. The reason: We won." In other words, Boutin contends that if one looks back at what music file-sharers have said publicly to justify their actions, going all the way back to the Napster days of 1999/2000, such as high prices, DRM [digital rights management], poor audio quality, record label exploitation, lack of deep catalogues, etc., that those rationales no longer exist. iTunes and Amazon sell high-bitrate DRM-free tracks at relatively low cost, have massive catalogues, and even allow more of the purchase price to go to the artists themselves. Ultimately, Boutin wants file-sharers to just admit that they have gotten everything they claimed to have wanted, and that the only reason left for pirating music is an indefensible one, that "You're cheap."

> *In the course of the post-Napster decade, we have come to recognize the profound economic implications of digital media interacting with the internet.*

While the article did generate a lot of angry comments and some more thoughtful responses, I think both Boutin and his vocal readers have missed some larger issues that go much deeper into the on-going dynamic of online music sharing, and explain why any declarations of its eminent demise are wishful thinking at best.

Free Music Online

To start, I don't think anyone should pay attention to what was said by Napster users, or by file-sharers in general about why they download music. Tens (maybe hundreds) of millions of people have downloaded an.mp3 at some point over the last decade, from every country on Earth with a connection to the internet. Why do they do it? Ultimately, unless one insists on seeing the phenomenon in purely moral terms, I don't think it really matters what people say publicly about why they refuse to purchase digital music. The fact is, millions of music fans choose to use Bittorrent, digital lockers, Usenet, etc. to get their music. And by their actions, they have created an economic dynamic that is much more important, and has far more long term implications, than endless debates about 128 kbps.mp3's versus FLAC's [different audio formats] or how exploitative the recording industry is.

In the course of the post-Napster decade, we have come to recognize the profound economic implications of digital media interacting with the internet, and not just in simple notions of "digitial distribution" or the "long tail." Instead, we now understand that because every single DRM scheme is inherently doomed to failure, and that the marginal cost of copying a digital media file is and will always be essentially zero, then we can only speak of digital media in a context of infinite supply. I am not a trained economist, but it is patently clear that an infinite good, available to anybody with a modem, will trend very quickly to a price of zero, no matter what the proponents of strict intellectual property regimes would prefer. While there is clearly a large number of people that purchase.mp3's (or AAC's) from iTunes and Amazon, they remain a distinct minority in a global online world that simply does not accept the notion of exchanging money for digital music. I would even say that iTunes customers most likely value the convenience and technical simplicity the shopping experience provided by Apple far more than any true sense of the specific "value" of the files they purchase.

Examined from a purely economic viewpoint, music file sharers are rational actors that pay for the things they consider of tangible value.

In fact, it is precisely this dynamic of infinite versus scarce goods that points to the future of digital media online. As Mike Masnick of Techdirt has so powerfully demonstrated, once content creators understand the problematics of trying to charge for infinite goods, they can truly embrace the countless possibilities of creating tangible goods, that cannot be copied and can be sold for real money. It is almost a cliche now to speak of how musicians can rely on live performances to substitute for sales of recordings, but that is merely the tip of the iceberg of what content creators can do, by creating non-replicable experiences that allow their fans to connect with the art and artists in ways that are truly worth treasuring.

The Ethics of Downloading

Streaming services like Spotify also indicate how music can remain a revenue generator in a world of infinite goods, by providing a service and convenience that is of true value even to customers not used to paying for the music they download. Just as Netflix does not have a single film or TV show that is not available online for download for free, but can still build a massive customer base by recommending and presenting video content in a manner that their users love and happily pay for.

So, music pirates are in fact "cheap" according to Boutin's perspective, which judges music downloading as immoral because it ignores the desires of content creators to charge for digital copies of their work. But outside of this moral framework, examined from a purely economic viewpoint, music file sharers are rational actors that pay for the things they consider of tangible value (iPods, laptops, Internet access, concert tickets, band t-shirts, streaming subscriptions, etc., etc.) and do not pay for the infinitely copyable. And unless the content industries and their government representatives somehow do the impossible, and turn the Internet into something it currently is not, then the future will continue overwhelmingly in that direction.

7

Illegal Downloads Are Bankrupting Record Labels

Aniruddh Bansal

Aniruddh Bansal writes about music for Metal Assault.

Illegal downloading is unethical and is causing undue harm to the music industry. An example of this is the bankruptcy of Roadrunner Records. Fans may believe that they support a group by attending a concert or buying a tee-shirt, but album sales are an important part of any band's revenues. By downloading free music, fans are harming the bands, the record labels, and the entire music industry.

This is an article I've wanted to write since as long as I can remember, because illegal music downloading is something that bothers me more than anything else pertaining to the music industry. Yesterday, the extremely sad news of Roadrunner Records shutting down their UK, Europe and Canada offices reverberated through the metal community like a massive earthquake. Numerous employees working at those label offices are now out of jobs, and artists on the label in those territories now seek new label homes. Who knows what's going to happen to the Roadrunner albums that were slated for release. Even though the news is not official and hasn't come from Roadrunner yet, the rumors have been strong enough, and I feel this is as apt an occasion as ever to finally write this piece.

First of all, let me tell you, it's not like I've never illegally downloaded music. But, I did it quite a number of years back, as a college kid living in India, a country which sees literally no distribution of heavy metal albums. I downloaded, not because I didn't have enough money, but simply because I had no access to those albums. On rare occasions, I found metal albums in stores, and I did my best to save money in order to buy them. I will never forget the moment when I showed my friends a couple of Iron Maiden CDs I had purchased, and most of them laughed at me for doing so, calling it a 'waste of money'. So I've practiced the act of buying music from very early on, and still do. Some might say, it's easy for me to speak against illegal downloading because as a reviewer I get legal access to all albums anyway. But if you're in any of my social networks, you know very well that despite getting almost every album for free, I still go out and buy the vinyl copy of al bums I really like.

Illegal Downloading Is Stealing

That being said, I can understand people in territories like India downloading music illegally, because of the lack of access to legit forms of the music. But when those in the US and Europe do it, I find it highly detestable and strongly disagree with their reasoning behind it. Albums from all kinds of bands are so easily available in physical and digital form, and there is really no excuse for not buying the albums. I constantly come across posts on social networks and public forums, wherein people brag about supporting a band by buying their shirts and concert tickets, and stating that as the reason for not needing to buy the actual CD or MP3 of that band's new album. I do not concur with it, at all.

In my opinion, if you're buying a band's shirt, you pay for a piece of cloth you're going to wear. If you buy a concert ticket, you pay for the live show the band is going to play for you. These things don't make up for the illegal download. If you're paying for those things, why not pay for the music you'll listen to repeatedly at home? Using a product without taking permission and without paying for it is called stealing, and I'm sorry to say, this downloading activity is also categorized as stealing, but ethics aside, it all comes down to the financial implications. Let me explain.

Bands will either release self-funded low quality recordings, or will stop recording new music completely.

People aren't willing to understand the fact that a lot of money goes into recording an album of professional sound quality, and that money is supposed to be recuperated from album sales. I've also heard people say, "All that money goes to the record label and the band hardly makes anything out of it, so why should I buy the album?" Again, wrong thinking. The money does go to the label, yes, but the band still makes something from it, and by not buying the album you're taking away even the little bit they would make. Plus, the money the label makes from the sale of a band's album is invested back into the band to fund their tours and promotion campaigns. The exact reverse also happens a lot of the time, where the label funds a band's recording budget, books them for a touring cycle to promote the album, and then the band owes money to the label, which is recovered from album sales. The lack of album sales is a huge hindrance in the smooth running of this process, and creates trouble for the band and the label concerned.

Bankrupting the Music Industry

You might argue that bands make money by selling things such as shirts, hoodies, patches, and other merchandise, but in my view, it's only a small percentage of their revenue model, and there are middlemen involved. Same thing with the concert ticket sales. Venues, promoters, booking agents, roadies and a lot of other people get paid before the band or label gets anything. Bands like Black Sabbath, Led Zeppelin, Metallica and Iron Maiden are millionaires today not because of shirts and concert tickets, but because they benefited from multi-platinum selling albums released early in their careers, during simpler times, when there was no internet and people actually bought albums.

I really fear for the music industry, and feel sad to predict that eventually more and more labels will meet the same fate as Roadrunner Records. They'll all run out of money and will end up being unable to support the bands on their roster. Bands will either release self-funded low quality recordings, or will stop recording new music completely. I'm sure they'll still write new music, purely for their own creative satisfaction, because they can't keep playing the same old tunes on every tour. You'll hear new music only in live performances, and all the illegal downloaders out there will be left with nothing to download, other than live bootlegs. Imagine that. Do you really want the music industry to come to that? I encourage you to start buying music, and tell your friends to do the same. I'm pretty sure my plea will fall on deaf ears and won't change anything, but even If you think twice before going to a torrent website and downloading your favorite band's new album next time, I think I've done what I aimed to do with this article. Thank you very much.

8

The Music Industry Has Failed to Adapt to Changing Technology

Laurie Fisher

Laurie Fisher is a public relations consultant.

When downloading became a reality on the web, the music industry had an opportunity to expand distribution. Instead, it fought against change, attempting to retain control and maintain a high profit margin. Eventually, however, this backfired on the music industry, causing the loss of CD sales as online downloading (both free and paid) continued to grow. The only chance for the music industry to recover is to abandon old practices and implement innovative methods that meet consumer demand.

Okay, so the archaic nature of the music industry and the steadfast refusal to adapt to the changes brought about by the internet may hardly be a new topic for discussion, but given recent events (namely [file storage and viewing website] MegaUpload being taken down), it is worth looking at how the music industry and record labels have reacted since the introduction of the internet.

What should have been a medium that allowed for cheaper distribution, new business models and an invigorated approach to discovering and nurturing talent has instead largely been somewhat of a hindrance to the major players, who seek to maintain the status quo and continue with the old way of doing business. Ultimately, this has been to their detriment as they're effectively competing with the groundswell of communities on the internet and in social media. But just how did the music industry screw itself so massively?

Record Labels Ignored the Benefits

The fact is that the digitisation of music and the arrival of the internet should have been a good thing for the music industry. Not only did it mean cheaper production, allowing labels to do away with expensive CDs and packaging, it also meant cheaper and more widespread distribution at 50 per cent of the cost of CDs. In *What You Really Need To Know About The Internet,* John Naughton gives a compressed history of digital audio, where he explains that when Napster came along in 1999, fans got a taste of the ease of downloading and sharing music. But the labels chose not to listen. Napster then spawned subsequent services—Limewire et al [and others] that far exceeded the rate at which the music industry was able to respond: positively or negatively.

Not only did the music industry fail to recognise the benefits afforded by the internet and sharing music online, they also spectacularly ignored the fact that this was exactly what fans wanted. They also failed to react at a time when they could have. When file sharing first started, it was restricted massively by the size of files and the speed of broadband to actually download these files. It was largely inaccessible to the populace, but had they predicted that the increase in appetite for instant music would occur alongside improving technology and broadband speeds, they could have got their houses in order to be ready when it did arrive.

What they have also seemingly consistently ignored is the appetite for music that the internet and social technologies has brought about. While the industry seems to focus on album sales as an indicator of the internet 'killing' music, this is the wrong place to focus. Indeed, album sales have been in steady decline since 2000.

Yet digital music sales are not diminishing, as in 2011 digital music sales exceeded physical sales. And while total album sales (including physical and digital) grew by 1.3 per cent from 2010 to 2011, in digital album sales exclusively, there was a huge 19.5 per cent of growth. So the internet is not proving the threat the music industry is claiming it is, nor does it seem to be hampering profits in the way that they claim.

The music industry is a greedy industry, led by capitalist motivations when all around it, its fans are embracing a collective medium that brings new opportunities.

Capitalist Models in a Collective Medium

Where the music industry seems to be failing most, is in the refusal to adapt their business models to reach the full revenue potential of the internet. The accusation leveled at Mega-Upload was that it was causing losses of up to £300 million, through lost sales across creative industries. While there is a fair amount of contention around how that figure was reached and how the lost sales can really be attributed, the fact is that those in the creative industries are attempting to bring down those that they deem to be doing wrong by them, instead of looking at the revenue potential that might come by collaborating with sites like this.

The music industry is a greedy industry, led by capitalist motivations when all around it, its fans are embracing a collective medium that brings new opportunities not only in access to music but also through collaboration. Were the industry heads to adjust their capitalist motivations and accept that just might not be the way to do things any more, they may instead reach a new, better way.

Again, we can look to history to prove this lesson. While collaboration, interpretation or elaboration upon an existing work may ultimately be seen as detrimental to the original artist, we can see otherwise in the example of literature. In 1652, the philosopher John Locke kept a commonplace book in a library. This was essentially a public book where different people could make notes or record passages from works they were reading. It was essentially an early form of crowdsourcing. Yet it didn't lead to a compromise of the original works. Remixing has its place in creative industries for centuries. It hasn't led to the demise of them.

For Their Own Gains

What's interesting is that when you consider all the accusations and lawsuits brought about by music labels against social technologies, they seem perfectly happy to gain from it on their own terms. This can be seen perhaps most starkly in the case of 31 of the world's largest record labels, filing a lawsuit against TubeFire—which allowed people to easily download videos from Youtube. The site was removed and $3 million in damages were sought. Juxtapose this with the fact that Universal Music and Sony BMG are the two highest earners on Youtube and it seems we have an unfair game being played.

> *The failure to work more openly with social networks . . . will impact the music industry massively.*

The labels are happy to use a social platform where they can easily generate revenue, but when a derivative of the site is launched, they bring out the heavies and have it removed. This is not the way social technologies function and it will surely ultimately be detrimental to the labels, as they are not playing the game in the right way, only taking and not providing, which is against the ecosystem of the internet and therefore not sustainable.

Failure to Collaborate with Social Networks

When Facebook launched their Open Graph last year [2011], a number of music partners were announced, including Spotify, Earbits, MOG and Slackr. When Facebook announced 60 new Open Graph apps this year, a number of music partners were announced, including Turntable.fm, Rhapsody and SoundCloud. On neither of these occasions was a record label on the list. Now of course while we can't know whether the labels sought this but were rejected by Facebook, it's hard to imagine Facebook turning down a collaboration opportunity with a major label.

The failure to work more openly with social networks or let's be honest, Facebook, will impact the music industry massively. Not only have they effectively missed out on free advertising (how much of your timeline is now filled with links to songs your friends are playing?) but also on revenue. Opening up on Facebook did not cause the demise of Spotify. Of course not. It did the exact opposite and they are now benefiting from over four million more users.

A Plug in the Ocean

The music industry is screwing themselves over with the sheer impossibility of what they are trying to do. By filing complaints against sites that host or link to copyrighted material, instead of adapting their copyright policies or collaborating with the communities on there, they are entering a never-ending fight that will only seek to damage their reputation and continually force them to give users what they want. Shutting down Napster didn't kill music sharing online. Indeed digital sales (not free downloads) continue to rise. If the increase in free digital downloads is occurring alongside a rise in paid downloads, then the music industry is creating a problem that doesn't need to be there.

What they should instead be doing is focusing on new ways to offer content, that fits with user's desires. Take the fact that our time online is now at a premium as we face a barrage of content. Sure, there is a significant group of people that will happily stream or download content for free, slowly and sometimes at a poorer quality. But there is also a significant group, who value their time, that are willing to pay for access to the music that they want, in return for a speedier service.

Spotify certainly isn't having any trouble getting people to pay for their service, despite there being a free, ad-supported version available. Either way, Spotify is winning and generating revenue in a way that (the majority of) record labels won't do because they have instead focused their attentions on an impossible struggle.

The simple fact remains that the old way of doing things no longer applies.

The might of the community is simply too strong for the music industry, and they seem doomed to ignore this.

SonicAngel—Doing It Right

The problem, of course, is not consistent across the entire music industry with smaller, younger labels emerging or adapting to make the most of the benefits available within social media and also develop new business models at the same time. The Belgian record label SonicAngel is a good example of this, though it's early days so the success of their model is yet to be proven. They are working with Massachusetts Institute of Technology to develop tools that effectively scan the web for new talent, so doing away with heavy investment in A&R [artists and repertoire] that is often bandied about by record labels as needed to nurture talent and justify their stance against downloading.

Further to this, they are also implementing a model that relies on the crowd, as opposed to trying to fight against it. Fans are given the option to buy shares in the artists, as well as voting on content uploaded by artists themselves, which gives the record label deeper insight into what their fans actually want. And SonicAngels are certainly not an isolated case, as other ventures such as CrowdBands are attempting to harness the collective to change the way music is found, funded and distributed.

This is exactly where the music industry needs to be headed. The simple fact remains that the old way of doing things no longer applies. And just as with every cultural or creative industry that has undergone a forced change through the evolution of technology, fear abounds. But just as these industries have undergone changes for hundreds of years that were initially seen as a threat, they didn't spell the end. Scribes hand-writing copies of books didn't kill literature, the printing press didn't kill literature, public libraries didn't kill literature, the internet didn't kill literature, ebooks didn't kill literature. None of the changes the music industry is undergoing means that it is a dying industry. Just that they may have to be less greedy and more amenable to change.

9

The Compact Disc Is Obsolete

John O'Connell

John O'Connell is a journalist for The National, *an online English-language newspaper published in the United Arab Emirates.*

The compact disc, or CD, as a music medium is slowly dying. This should come as no surprise: technological change has been a constant in the music industry from the very beginning. Music is no longer looked at as a physical product to be owned, and consumers are turning away from CD collecting as it decreases in value.

It all started one weekend when some friends, Jim and Tessa, came over for dinner. I asked what they'd been doing all day. Jim answered for both of them: "We've been throwing away CDs," he said. "We're working our way through them alphabetically." As he explained it, his role in the exercise involved quality assessment—working out whether a CD was something they'd realistically ever listen to again. If he decided it was, he handed it to Tessa to feed into their new 3TB external hard drive; if it wasn't, he tossed it into the "charity shop" box. "There's no point selling them," said Jim. "They're completely worthless." (While this is an overstatement, it's certainly true that CDs, even limited pressings done for a band's fan club, have nothing like the value they had a decade ago—just look on eBay or Amazon Marketplace.)

Storage Problems

This was astonishing news. Jim was famous for his CD collection, which ran into the thousands and occupied vast stretches of prime shelf space. He had devoted most of his adult life to growing it, and no visit to his flat was complete without a listening session and tour of its outer reaches. How could he bring himself to do something so brutal?

"It isn't brutal," he protested. "It's a humane cull. Just think of all the CDs you never play any more. I bet you've got loads." He walked over to my shelves and pulled a few CDs out at random. "Take this Turin Brakes one. You bought it because you liked that strummy song about having WD40 in your veins. But did you listen to any of the other tracks?" I shook my head.

"Well then. Oh hang on, what's this? That Elvis Costello album with the string quartet—The Juliet Letters. I bought this, too. It's awful, isn't it? Really boring and worthy. Chuck it out. As for this . . ." He pulled out Aquarium by the Danish-Norwegian popsters Aqua. "I remember you buying this, back in 1997 or whenever it was. You said it was a 'post-ironic Europop masterpiece'. It wasn't, was it? Don't look like that—you can feed 'Barbie Girl' into iTunes before tossing it."

Music was like air and didn't require any sort of physical complement.

In fact, Jim is not alone. CD disposal (or recycling) has become commonplace among thirtysomethings scared of being trapped somewhere between the past and the future—and worried about how much junk they seem to have acquired. For many expats, an accumulation of CDs—stashed away in an attic back home, or crammed into an expensive storage facility—is a problem that waits to be dealt with.

"I have at least 200 CDs in my parents' garage," admits 28-year-old Stuart Turnbull, a Dubai-based marketing executive who moved from the UK a year ago. "The cost of shipping them was prohibitive, and most of the music is on my iPod anyway. I tried to sell a few on Amazon's second-hand trading site, but I got so little money for them I gave up. I know it's only a matter of time before my parents tell me I have to get rid of them."

New Technology

The writing has been on the wall for CDs since at least 2001, the year Fortune magazine got so excited about Apple and its "new kind of gadget that has the potential to change how we think about personal audio-entertainment gizmos". Of course, the iPod did more than that. It cemented the idea that music was like air and didn't require any sort of physical complement—no case or sleeve; no artwork beyond a tiny picture on a screen; no sleevenotes or detailed track information. (So you want to know which musicians played on a given track, or who produced it? Tough. Look it up on the internet.)

When the beleaguered record label EMI relaunched The Beatles' back catalogue with shiny new remastered editions in 2008, the basic quality of the packaging was noted by critics. But then why would you bother mimicking, say, the original Sergeant Pepper sleeve (as the 1987-vintage, first-generation CD did) when you know that hardly anyone is going to be paying attention?

Jim's external hard drive will soon look as clunky as the eight-track cartridge player my father used to have in his car.

For many, though, CDs and vinyl records aren't just "sound carriers" but emotional totems. Like photographs, they evoke powerful memories. (Where did you buy that Nirvana album? Who were you dating at the time? Where were you living?) It follows, then, that throwing away a CD should be like tearing up a photograph. So why isn't it?

The problem for the CD, invented in the late 1970s by Philips and Sony and introduced in 1982, is that it has no aesthetic appeal: it isn't a beautiful object in the way that a vinyl record was, especially in vinyl's 1970s heyday when gatefold sleeves and lavish artwork were all the rage. (Think of the graphic designer Storm Thorgerson's extraordinary work with Pink Floyd.) Even when a CD has emotional significance, it remains easy to disparage as "podfood" because it looks disposable.

Last year, Sony Japan announced that it would no longer be making that 1980s icon the cassette Walkman—which shocked those of us who thought they'd stopped years ago. The cassette tape's demise was linked to its poor sound quality. But in their defence, CDs still sound great compared to MP3s. A future-proof, loss-less form of compression that doesn't take up loads of memory has yet to be invented. Convert your CDs into MP3s or even superior-sounding AAC files (the type used by Apple) and even if you're no audiophile, you'll notice the difference in quality, especially when they're played on a high-end docking station.

Ambitious and futuristic though it sounds, Jim's transferring-CDs-to-a-hard-drive plan still cleaves to the romantic idea that music is something you own physically, even if it's in the form of digital files. Within several years, say trend analysts, not only will a locket-sized MP3 player be able to hold 250,000 songs in its terabyte memory, but music will either be streamed into our homes à la Spotify or stored somewhere in the "cloud", ie on the internet. Jim's external hard drive will soon look as clunky as the eight-track cartridge player my father used to have in his car.

I pointed this out to him, but he didn't seem to mind. "I don't care," he said. "I just want the shelf space back."

10

The Compact Disc Is
Not Obsolete

Brian Boyd

Brian Boyd is a journalist for the Irish Times.

A recent story in the magazine Side-Line *predicted the imminent death of the compact disc (CD). No major record label, however, would go on the record in regard to the future of the CD. In reality, predicting the demise of the CD is premature. While the availability of music online has changed the music industry, many consumers still prefer and buy CDs. Although online music will continue to eat away at CD sales, the CD itself is far from dead.*

It was inevitable. The report went like this. By the end of next year the major record labels are planning to have abandoned the CD and replaced it with downloads and streams through iTunes and similar music services. That's because the CD is an anachronism from a pre-online era, according to the online music magazine *Side-Line*. CDs won't disappear completely, the report continued, but the format will occupy as small a niche as vinyl does now. Its end not only makes economic sense, as downloads are cheaper than a physical product to provide, but is also in tune with how we consume music in these days of the smartphone and the tablet.

The story was widely blogged and tweeted, and almost everyone accepted that technological progress had lapped the physical CD and that we were going to live our cultural life happily ever after in the cloud.

The Rise of Online Music

There's just one problem with the *Side-Line* story: it's wrong. At first it looked solid: more and more people are opting for downloads, and CDs have the drawback, when they don't sell as well as expected, of leaving retailers and record labels with return and storage costs. Downloads, on the other hand, incur no packaging, transport or storage costs and minimal distribution costs.

What if the end is not nigh for the CD? And what if that means our cultural future will not be entirely digital?

Music stores have been giving CDs less and less floor space in recent years, as video games are now the big sellers on the high street. More people are getting their music from iTunes and other digital services, and a whole generation of music consumers each own hundreds of albums but have never touched a CD.

After *Side-Line* published its story, people started to wonder about magazines, books and films. Surely, the argument ran, if it's cheaper, easier and more convenient to acquire music, books and films online, we're looking at the end not only of the CD but also of physical copies of books and films as well.

But what if the end is not nigh for the CD? And what if that means our cultural future will not be entirely digital? *Side-Line* contacted three major labels—Universal, EMI and Sony—about its story, but all declined to comment. That probably fuelled a grassy-knoll theory [conspiracy, after the assassination of US president John F. Kennedy] that the majors had privately decided to kill off the CD next year but didn't want the news to be reported too soon.

The Real Future of Music

This week, at least, it was easy to find music-industry people who will talk about the future of the compact disc. The International Federation of the Phonographic Industry represents the interests of the recording industry worldwide, and CD sales are its lifeblood. "This story was first written back in October, and as far as I can see it hasn't gained any credibility at all," says Adrian Strain, the federation's director of communications. "CDs still account for more than 60 per cent of industry revenues globally—more than 70 per cent in some markets, such as Germany—and there is still healthy consumer demand for the physical product. This is despite the rapid growth we have seen in the industry's digital revenues."

Gennaro Castlado, a spokesman for HMV, says, "I don't think we should write off the CD just yet, as there are still a huge number of people who like the idea of owning and collecting music in physical formats, especially when they can make their own digital copies to get the best of both worlds. There will be a viable market for CDs for quite a while to come."

Universal, the world's biggest record label, says it has no intention of stopping production of CDs, pointing out that discs have made up 72 per cent of album sales in the UK and Ireland this year. If you look at last week's Irish album chart, you will find that the number-one album, *Christmas* by Michael Bublé, sold 10,610 copies, of which only 654 were digital copies.

Domino records, home to artists such as Arctic Monkeys and King Creosote, is one of the biggest independent labels. Its director, John Dyer, says, "I've just been looking at the digital sales for Susan Boyle. They amount to 0.5 per cent of her total sales. The other 99.5 per cent is for CD sales. What you get with a lot of these stories about new technology killing off old formats is an incredibly American- and UK-centric view of the world. I know of certain European territories where the people are just culturally averse to using their credit card online to buy a download. Spain, to take just one example, doesn't really go for the digital format."

The CD Consumer

Susan Boyle illustrates where the story about the supposed demise of the CD was right. The people who buy her music tend not to use smartphones or iTunes. The same is broadly true for classical recordings and for country music and rock'n'roll, all of which appeal to an older, CD-buying audience.

The CD is safe for now. A large section of us, for whatever reason—economic, social or personal taste—will always prefer the tangible product.

With more contemporary genres, the gap between digital and physical sales is narrowing. Over the next few years, CDs will become less important in sales of pop, hip hop, urban, and r'n'b, as teenage music fans are already used to the one-click model of getting music.

Age alone isn't the defining factor. Certain types of consumers demand the physical album, book or film. They enjoy the tactile sensation, the artwork and the way the objects are presented. People also like to look at and organise their collections, not just move them around a desktop with a mouse.

The CD-is-dead theory also assumes that people can afford high-speed broadband or that they can easily spend €500 on new devices. The drift to digital will continue because of its convenience and its generally more competitive prices. But the CD is safe for now. A large section of us, for whatever reason—economic, social or personal taste—will always prefer the tangible product.

Why CDs Still Rock

They look great: Granted, they are made of unlovely plastic, but they are shiny and, even after three decades, look futuristic. And the music they hold is read by lasers. Which is still very *Tomorrow's World* [a BBC television series focusing on science and technology].

The sonic experience: Yes, audiophile anoraks might think music should be listened to only on a beach at midnight surrounded by scented candles and only on vinyl. But, for the rest of us, the CD does the job just fine.

You can freeze them: Apparently, if you put your CDs into a freezer for a few days the result is superior sound quality. It can also remove scratches.

The album sleeves: Never as big as with vinyl, but with a CD at least there's a bit of art to it. Downloads have made the album cover almost invisible.

Arts and crafts: You can make sculptures from them. I once made a beautiful shiny fish from a Westlife [Irish band] CD.

11

The Album Format
Is Obsolete

Guardian

The Guardian *is a British newspaper covering world events and culture.*

The album is quickly giving way to the individual track. The reason is simple: when iTunes allowed music fans to buy individual tracks separately, the album format began to suffer. It was a trend in progress, first suggested by the CD in the 1980s. Fans could easily skip or repeat tracks, spoiling the continuity of an album. While the album may no longer have the same prestige, it is an art form worth preserving.

This summer has seen the loss of many greats: the King of Pop [Michael Jackson], the king of psyche-garage-pop (Sky Saxon) and arguably the finest of British rock journalists, Steven Wells. I can surely be forgiven for failing to realise that the album died at the same time.

"Albums are dead," declared the Cult's Ian Astbury, no less, to the *El Paso Times* last month. "The format is dead. ITunes destroyed albums—the whole idea of the album. Nobody buys albums, it's been proven."

Astbury went on to tell journalist Doug Pullen of his admiration for Radiohead: "I find their albums highly listenable. I get lost in a body of work." But in the main, his point seemed to be that we may as well just leave the LP to draw its last breath.

The most recognisable part of Beethoven's Ninth is the Scherzo. Perhaps it doesn't suit our flighty 21st-century existence to drop out for more than an hour to listen to the full symphony. Why bother wasting time on the whole of *Dark Side of the Moon* when Money alone will do?

The speed with which pundits have been kissing the album goodnight has only grown since the mass adoption of the MP3.

From Album to CD

The album proper, some say, began in 1956 with Peggy Lee's Black Coffee, for which the songs were carefully chosen and ordered rather than thrown together. The Beatles' *Rubber Soul* and the Beach Boys' *Pet Sounds* marked the dawn of the golden era, and rock groups were divided by critics into "singles" and "albums" bands. The most versatile and successful acts swung both ways, but for some, only a 20-minute, vinyl-side excursion into the centre of the mind would suffice. The album was a trip, and you had to do the whole thing.

The album was dealt its first blow by Dire Straits. Forgive them, for they know not what they did. In 1985, their digitally recorded full-length release *Brothers in Arms* was the first to sell a million copies on CD. And, for the first time, UK album-buyers were able to easily flick their way past tracks that bored them, without having to move the stylus by hand and avoid losing the Blu-tacked coin that weighted it down. These new optical-disc consumers could also ignore the rest of *Brothers in Arms*, if they desired, and stick the 8.26-minute-long hit "Money for Nothing" on repeat ad infinitum (if you had the vinyl version, it was shortened to 7.04).

Enter the MP3

The speed with which pundits nave been kissing the album goodnight has only grown since the mass adoption of the

MP3 as music format of choice. Last November [2008], the rock writer Chuck Klosterman claimed Guns N' Roses' *Chinese Democracy* would be "the last album that will be marketed as a collection of autonomous-but-connected songs, the last album that will be absorbed as a static manifestion of who the band supposedly is, and the last album that will matter more as a physical object than as an internet sound file. This is the end of that."

I'm not sure Klosterman has been proven right just yet. The recent excitement over the Mercury prize shortlist shows that an award that celebrates the album, rather than just a few tracks by an artist, continues to be relevant.

However, many reviews now recommend just a few songs to download, leaving the others—the so-called filler tracks, many of which improve with time—to languish in obscurity. Surely now is the time for a counter-revolution. Failing a neo-Luddite [those who oppose technology] crusade to destroy the shuffle and track-skip capabilities of every MP3 player in the world, we must promote the virtues of the album as a whole. The single-track counter-revolution begins here: we don't just want the chocolate fancies in the window, we want the whole bloody bakery!

12

Singles Will Not Eclipse Albums

Moses Avalon

Moses Avalon is a writer and consultant in the music industry, as well as the author of Million Dollar Mistakes *and* Confessions of a Record Producer.

Although popular opinion states that the CD has given way to the single download at iTunes and other online stores, the reality is far different. Once iTunes began offering albums as units, albums sold equally well. Likewise, performers like Kid Rock and AC/DC have initially issued albums in CD-only format, proving that consumers will still buy CDs in large quantities. Even independent labels that sell fewer copies than major labels frequently sell the majority of their albums in the CD format. While the availability of downloading singles has changed the music market, the album is far from dead.

You hear story after story of people illegally downloading MP3 singles off the Internet. Who steals CDs from record stores anymore? Well, like most things, when you drill down the answer gets more interesting.

A better hypothetical question might be: Imagine two bins: One has CD singles and the other has CD albums. If nobody was watching, which bin would be emptied out quicker due to theft?

Ah . . . rephrased this way, the answer seems a bit more gray. And it is.

There has never been a definitive objective test of the public's preference. The market research surveys that can help us here tell us that people enjoy buying more than one song at a time, and it makes sense that if they are going to buy several songs by the same artist, then it should be an album—which traditionally means a CD.

Until the mid-1960s everyone bought singles. Then labels introduced collections of singles on one large "long-playing" record, called an LP. But, with the "singles market" revitalized again due to iTunes and P2P [file sharing programs], the public, for the first time in history, will get to decide the bundling (or un-bundling) of music instead of Execs, accountants, managers, and even the artists. And what does the public want. . .?

CDs and the Cloud

The votes so far seem to indicate a split decision. While singles are clearly a choice for the young or those new to the technology, as soon as iTunes began to offer albums, people began to buy them with almost the same fervor as singles.

Labels are going to begin insisting that marque acts be sold exclusively on CD for the first few months or "album only" in digital stores.

In addition, cloud based digital "music lockers" may create a new need for CDs. Labels are trying to enforce restrictions on the types of files that can be loaded into these new services for fear that these same services might encourage theft. These restrictions will likely include terms stating that only those songs purchased legally, via CD and through approved vendors such as iTunes, Amazon, etc. are allowed to be uploaded on these premium cloud services.

Given the wholesale nature of the music locker concept, people might increasingly turn to mediums that naturally grouped songs together *legally* under one license, for easy upload—the CD or digital album.

Big Stars Will Ride the Market

Another influencing factor is that labels are going to begin insisting that marque acts be sold exclusively on CD for the first few months or "album only" in digital stores. In fact, this has already happened, but you probably didn't hear about it.

In 2008 AC/DC and Kid Rock, two of that year's biggest rock acts, insisted on CD "album-only" sales. Did this insistence pay off? Yep.

Kid Rock's label decided to forgo a digital release altogether and released *Rock N Roll Jesus* only on CD. It wasn't until a year had past, and over 1.7 million albums had sold, that they finally issued a digital license to Amazon MP3 to sell the record but in an "album only" format. Oddly absent from his chosen digital retailers is iTunes who were excluded by Kid Rock as they don't allow artists to sell complete albums in the "album only" format. Kid Rock's *Rock N Roll Jesus* was one of the top five albums of that year and has sold over 5 million units to date.

And AC/DC's *Black Ice* album was released exclusively on CD and was only available at Wal-Mart (in North America), and trailed right behind Kid Rock's as the fourth best-selling album of 2008, with 1.6 million copies sold. It charted number 1 in over 29 countries and has since shipped over 6 million copies . . . and not one of those copies was a single or a download.

Okay, that was 3 years ago: a lifetime in the world of digital music distribution. And then here come the hip, Facebook generation "experts." Many claimed that Rock and AC/DC left a lot of money on the table by denying digital sales of singles. Their consensus seemed to feel that this type of "old school" move is only achievable by larger acts with very strong followings. A newer act wouldn't dare experiment with this type of strategy.

They were and are still wrong.

Independent CD Releases

In the indie world, sites like Bandcamp claim that their artists' albums to singles sales are on a 6:1 ratio in CD albums favor. And in the major label land, their entire music business economy is based on the album configuration and that will not change anytime soon. Artist advances are inextricably designed around and connected to the album format. A fact kept from the public.

So my money says expect to see more "album only" demands for new releases by those artists that can see the writing on the wall and afford to alienate [a] few die-hard singles-only fans.

Yet, another reason albums will survive for quite some time; albums are cool! It's a cohesive, 50-minute sound vision. Singles were created as an economic reality of selling albums, not as a substitute for them.

Albums live! And for now, the sales numbers prove it.

And as for albums in CD form, we can be sure that the CD format is not going to die anytime soon if we just look at the number of new CD players/recorders manufactured every day: well over 100,000! We use these players/recorders to archive favorite releases which helps ensure the format's place . . . at least for the near future.

The Haters

Technology innovators like Steve Jobs, don't care about the integrity of music as art. No human who invented the best way to buy, catalog, and "share" music as individual tracks, can be a real fan of music as an art form. (Sorry Steve, I love your brain, but your heart. . . ?)

I remember trying to get my mother to join the iPod generation years ago by telling her that it could hold her entire Classical collection. She said "But it cuts up the symphony into little bits." (old iPods/iTunes used to treat movements as if they were singles and wouldn't play them seamlessly.) I was ashamed. My mother "got it" long before I did: music is about creativity, not the technology you play it on. Anyone who tries to tell you otherwise is a music hater, even if they don't know it. They have sold their souls to the tech-gods if they truly believe that artists should start making three-minute singles and forget about their album vision just because a digital retailer has decided that music is easier to sell in bite sized chunks. That's what radio tried to do to music, but albums survived that effort and they will survive this one too.

Music lives! Albums live! And for now, the sales numbers prove it.

13

Vinyl Records Are Making a Comeback

Brian Passey

Brian Passey writes for USA Today *and also reports for* The Spectrum *in St. George, Utah.*

While many independent record stores have seen a decline in CD sales, they have also witnessed a renewed interest in vinyl records. In 2010, records were the fastest growing format, helping bolster the bottom line of many struggling independent record stores. Lovers of vinyl also argue that records sound warmer than CDs. Surprisingly, perhaps, those most attracted to vinyl are the youth market, or those who did not grow up with records.

As both a music lover and record store owner, Tim Cretsinger is excited about the recent resurgence of vinyl record albums.

"This is my favorite thing to do—hold a batch of records like this," Cretsinger, owner of Groovacious in Cedar City, Utah, says as he hugged a stack of new records close to his chest. "It reminds me of the old days."

Vinyl Makes a Comeback

According to recent Nielsen SoundScan numbers, vinyl was the fastest-growing musical format in 2010, with 2.8 million units sold, the format's best year since SoundScan began tracking sales in 1991.

Vinyl's increase in popularity is providing a beacon of hope for independent record stores—an industry that has suffered with the increase of digital downloads this past decade.

When Cretsinger moved his business from Keiser, Ore., to Cedar City in 2000 there were two other record stores in the college town of about 28,000. Now, the closest independent record store is in Las Vegas, 175 miles away.

"Vinyl seems to be the light at the end of the tunnel for those of us who have hung in there," he says. "It's kind of a surprising light at the end of the tunnel. It's incredibly exciting."

Listening to music on a vinyl record is an event. It forces listeners to sit down at a turntable and listen to the music.

Back to the Basics

Not only have vinyl album sales picked up, but the interest in record players has increased as well. Cretsinger said he got tired of directing his customers to other businesses where they could purchase turntables, so he began offering a small selection at his store in January.

Like Groovacious, Plan 9 Music stores in Richmond and Charlottesville, Va., are fairly new to the turntable market, but have offered vinyl records since the first store opened in 1981, says owner Jim Bland. Although he never quit selling vinyl, Bland says sales were slow for many years as CDs dominated the market.

However, as CD sales plummeted in recent years, Plan 9 Music found itself with some open space on the floor. That empty space is now back to the basics.

"It's filled in with vinyl," Bland says.

As a way to promote their businesses, 700 independent record stores across the nation have joined together since 2008 to celebrate Record Store Day on the third Saturday of April. Record Store Day regularly features limited-edition CDs and vinyl records available only at independent retailers.

"Last year all the cool stuff was vinyl," Bland says. "People were lining up to get it."

A Better Sound

Like Record Store Day itself, Cretsinger says, listening to music on a vinyl record is an event. It forces listeners to sit down at a turntable and listen to the music, giving them an opportunity to enjoy the cover art and read the liner notes.

"There's something organic and historical about playing music that way," he says. "It sounds better."

The scratches and pops often associated with the vinyl sound are all part of the "warmth" Cretsinger and other record store owners such as John Kunz, of Waterloo Records in Austin, say vinyl offers.

Kunz says CDs are more convenient than vinyl and easier to manage, so they had their place in the music industry for a time. However, Kunz sees a change in his customers' taste from the digital sound of Internet downloads to what the classic vinyl format offers.

The music lovers buying these records aren't necessarily those who grew up with them in the 1960s and 1970s.

"I think there was a pendulum swing back to the analog sound," he says. "It's sound waves rather than zeroes and ones emulating a sound wave."

Terry Currier, owner of Music Millennium in Portland, Ore., says vinyl aficionados treat their passion as art, as opposed to a product.

"People didn't interact with CDs the way they did with vinyl," Currier says. "I think people lost that interaction they had with the vinyl."

Vinyl Lovers

The music lovers buying these records aren't necessarily those who grew up with them in the 1960s and 1970s. Record store owners across the nation say teenagers and young adults constitute a large portion of their vinyl customers.

"There are tweens, teens and twentysomethings looking through Mom and Dad's record collection," he says. "All of a sudden Mom and Dad are a lot cooler than the kid might have expected."

Currier says it's almost like vinyl appreciation skipped a generation. Now purchasing vinyl is "cool" for younger customers because it's "retro." For the youngest of the customers, it might even be something their parents never experienced.

Bland agrees: "It's cool; it's hip. My 14-year-old's even getting into it."

Among Cretsinger's customers at Groovacious in Cedar City is Matthew Montgomery, a 25-year-old Web developer, freelance music journalist and student at Southern Utah University. Montgomery says he began to seriously get into vinyl about two years ago, and now it's practically his exclusive musical format.

He says there is an "aesthetic difference" in the sound of vinyl records compared with the digital downloads purchased by many others of his generation.

Even Best Buy seems to have noticed the popularity of vinyl records.

The Vinyl Resurgence

"I think vinyl is incredibly exciting," Montgomery says. "To see a resurgence in it is beautiful."

Montgomery says the act of walking into a record store to purchase his music is part of vinyl's allure as well.

"To me that represents a cultural idea that is incredibly attractive," he says. "It's a place you can explore and learn and talk to people."

While vinyl sales help independent stores stand apart from nationwide retail chains, even Best Buy seems to have noticed the popularity of vinyl records.

About 100 Best Buy stores now carry a small selection of new and classic albums following a test period that began in the fall of 2008, says Best Buy spokeswoman Erin Bix. Best Buy also offers 14,000 vinyl titles online.

14

Digital and Analog Audio Formats Each Have Pros and Cons

Zak Claxton

Zak Claxton is the stage name of Jeff Klopmeyer, who is a Los Angeles-based singer-songwriter, performing musician, and small business owner.

One of the longstanding arguments in music circles centers on the issue of sound quality: is analog better than digital? Or, stated in more down-to-earth terms, do vinyl records sound better than CDs and MP3s? One major advantage of digital is cost. Recording music on analog tape is very expensive; recording digital music on a typical home computer, on the other hand, is inexpensive. While many people argue that vinyl/analog sounds warmer, almost everyone today listens to CDs and MP3 files. In truth, the quality of sound is subjective.

Most of the people who read this blog know me as a guy who strums a guitar and sings, and you're correct. That's what I am, but it's not the only thing I am. I'm also someone's dad. I'm someone's significant other. I'm a guy who owns and operates a small marketing communications company. And while my background and my career has always been integrated with the music world, a good portion of my actual education was in the technical side of audio recording and music production. While I've always been a performing musician—nearly my entire life—I also spent a good amount of time on what we call "the other side of the glass", meaning that I've engineered and produced music.

As you would imagine, there are entire communities that revolve around the art and science of audio recording, and no single aspect of recording has been as divisive as the argument of "digital versus analog". Even today, some 28 years after the Compact Disc ushered in digital audio to the masses, nothing starts a good 10-page thread on audio forums than someone opining about their preferences and reasons for choosing one over the other. I thought it might be nice to talk about this a little and explain the fast version of why this remains such a hot topic.

1. Analog Sounds Better

"Sounds better" is a stupid thing to write. Listening to music recording is subjective, meaning that what I like might not be what you like. However, without getting into the science behind it, most people prefer the sound of a song that was well recorded on analog tape than those recorded via digital systems, and most people prefer the sound of music being played back on a clean vinyl LP record than from a CD or especially from an MP3 file. Analog simply represents a better approximation of the original sounds being recorded, and there's a warmth and depth to analog that digital recordings fail to completely achieve.

What people can do by recording with digital audio workstations . . . is simply amazing.

---

2. Analog Doesn't Sound Better

All this nostalgic talk about analog sounding so much better than digital leaves out one key element: the tangible act of playing back music! Records almost immediately get scratches, and often even the new ones have clicks and pops that happen in the manufacturing process. Cassette tapes were never a good format for listening to music; the noise floor of a cassette meant that when you turned it up during quiet moments, you always heard the hiss of the tape. So while it's great in theory, it's not always great in practice.

3. Analog Is Expensive

Whooo boy. Below, you'll see me holding a reel of 2″ tape that I used for a 24-track recording back in the early '90s. The machine that I used to record this music was an MCI JH-24, which at the time cost around $50,000. But let's say you don't need the machine; you just need the tape. A reel like the one I'm holding below currently costs about $500. Running at standard speeds, that reel will hold maybe two songs' worth of music. The amount of tape needed for a full album ends up being about $2500 or more. That's fine if you're a wealthy rock star, but for typical people who just want to record, the cost is way too prohibitive.

4. Digital Offers More Creative Tools

It's not even debatable. What people can do by recording with digital audio workstations (i.e., computers) is simply amazing. I can copy and paste audio tracks. I can add processing that simply plugs into the recording software I use. I can change the pitch and timing of a performance as needed. While some of these things were possible on analog tape, the process that was required to achieve them was incredibly time consuming, and could ruin an entire recording with one small error (as opposed to hitting the "undo" command when you screw up).

5. Digital Is Convenient

It would take me pages and pages to explain "the old way" of recording and distributing music. First, you didn't do it. It was a process reserved for musicians/bands that were signed to record labels, who would invest the thousands of dollars it took to go into a recording studio and create singles and albums. Then, the master recording was sent to a plant—there weren't very many of them—where albums were pressed and sent to stores. And to sell the music, people had to physically go to the store and buy the album.

Today, a skilled person can make a professionally recorded album in his/her bedroom on a pretty typical computer, and their song can be made available around the world via services like iTunes. My "tape" is the amount of space on my hard drive, and with the price of large drives continuing to dwindle, it's easy to do an entire album on a drive that costs maybe $100. The person buying the music can do so by clicking a mouse and entering a credit card number. While the process of opening the world of professional recording has its downsides (like a lot of people being able to release less-than-spectacular music), I can't help but be in favor of something that democratizes a process that used to be reserved for the wealthy elite.

There's no clear cut winner in this now-old argument, and the act of arguing about it is a massive waste of time.

---

6. Everyone Listens To Digital Playback Systems Anyway

I'll get yelled at for writing that, but it's really true. How do you listen to music? If you're like 95% of people in 2011, you listen to digital audio downloads like MP3 or AAC files you buy online, or you listen to CDs. Whether it's your iPod, your car stereo, or even the radio, almost every playback system you hear today is digital based. Even with those old records that were recorded in analog before the digital revolution, you are almost certainly listening to newer digital remasters by now.

One good piece of news for analog lovers: due to a couple of different factors, the use of turntables and vinyl LPs has actually had a resurgence over the past 7–8 years, and more artists—especially indie musicians like myself—are opting to do runs of record pressings of their new recordings. While I can't justify the cost of doing this for my own music (I don't sell enough albums to break even on it), the idea is constantly tempting. I find that I yearn for the day of hearing the needle plop down on some fresh vinyl and hearing my own recordings come out of the speakers. And I'm not alone; the recent Foo Fighters album *Wasting Light* was completely recorded on analog tape and is offered in an LP version. The reason for this was that Dave Grohl and his band were adamant that they wanted a rock album that sounded as good as music can be experienced, and I applaud their effort; it was worth it.

So, Which One Is Better?

Both . . . and neither. There's no clear cut winner in this now-old argument, and the act of arguing about it is a massive waste of time. No one is going to be convinced, be it through scientific explanations or evangelizing the subjective sound of one over the other, that the opposite side is correct. The good news in all of this is that while digital audio isn't ever going away, it does continue to evolve and improve, and there may come a point in the not-distant future that audibly, one will be indistinguishable from the other. Until then, as I always say, the most important part of making good music is writing good songs . . . a much better use of someone's time than arguing about the technological side of things.

15

Online Music Listening Extends the Possibilities of Traditional Radio

Sasha Frere-Jones

Sasha Frere-Jones is a music journalist and critic writing for the New Yorker, Spin, and other publications.

Increasingly, fans are relying on web-based services to choose or help choose music selections. With sites like Pandora, playlists are built around the listeners choices in a number of categories; with sites like Spotify, listeners create playlists or use those created by other listeners. Either way, music consumption today is beginning to resemble our previous reliance on the old-fashioned radio d.j., adding a touch of chance to the listening experience.

No one knows what the future of the music business will look like, but the near future of *listening* to music looks a lot like 1960. People will listen, for free, to music that comes out of a stationary box that sits indoors. They'll listen to music that comes from an object that fits in the hand, and they'll listen to music in the car. That box was once a radio or a stereo; now it's a computer. The handheld device that was once a plastic AM radio is now likely to be a smart phone. The car is still a car, though its stereo now plays satellite radio and MP3s. But behind the similarities is a series of subtle shifts in software and portability that may relocate the experience of listening—even if nobody has come close to replacing the concept of the radio d.j., whose job lingers as a template for much software.

"Of the twenty hours a week that an average American spends listening to music, only three of it is stuff you own. The rest is radio," Tim Westergren told me. Westergren is the founder of Pandora, one of several firms that have brought the radio model to the Internet. Pandora offers free, streaming music, not so different from the radio stations that many people grew up with, except that the d.j. is you, more or less. The company does not sell music—like normal radio, Internet radio is considered a promotional tool for recordings, even though the fees that it pays to labels are currently higher than those paid by terrestrial stations.

Pandora is acting like a radio station, not like a replacement for a potential sale—you can't keep skipping until it plays what you want.

If you go to Pandora, on the Web or on a phone, you begin by picking a song or an artist, which then establishes a "station." Pandora's proprietary algorithm [a set of rules for solving a problem], in which a panel of musicians assesses about four hundred variables, like "bravado level in vocals" and "piano style," for each song, leads you from what you chose to a song that seems to fit with it, musically. You also have the option to teach the algorithm, by giving a song a thumbs up or a thumbs down. The company has captured a very large chunk of the Internet-radio audience—the service now has fifty million users, who listen an average of more than eleven hours a month.

The Pandora experience isn't much like being guided by a d.j. on a radio station—at least, not yet. (That delicious unpredictability is now approximated by the thousands of mixtapes and podcasts that are released by individuals on the Web, free of charge, every day.) I started my station with Public Image Ltd's "Poptones," a 1979 song that is loaded with bass, dissonant guitar, and the sinus bray of John Lydon, once known as Johnny Rotten. The band's sound is deeply indebted to reggae—the original bassist was named Jah Wobble—but I couldn't make a reggae song appear on my Poptones station. I did get lots of bands I like: the Minutemen, the Birthday Party, and Fugazi, who all make aggressive music that, like Public Image's, is heavy on articulate rhythm and acidic guitar.

After skipping six songs, I received this message on my iPhone app: "Sorry, our music licenses force us to limit the number of songs you may skip." Pandora is acting like a radio station, not like a replacement for a potential sale—you can't keep skipping until it plays what you want.

On a recent car trip I took through Florida, Pandora was perfect: I plugged in my phone, hit a couple of buttons, and was rewarded with ninety minutes of instrumental hip-hop.

Music on Demand

The most popular alternative to the broadcast model is "on demand," which usually charges a subscription fee in return for the ability to choose exactly which song you'd like to hear. In Europe, the most prominent such service is Spotify, a Swedish company that has grown rapidly in the past year. In America, where Spotify has yet to debut, one of the biggest on-demand players is MOG, a new service that offers a wide array of listening options, the least expensive of which costs five dollars a month. MOG offers the option of streaming 320-kilobyte-per-second files, the highest available digital quality, though customers have been reluctant to pay extra for greater audio fidelity.

With MOG, you can play entire albums, create playlists, or let the service perform the same kind of algorithmic radio function that Pandora provides. (While listening to a song, you pull a slider all the way to the right; the software suggests related artists and tracks.) You can also share playlists with other users. I looked up the German rock band Can, and saw, on the right side of my Web browser, a small box called "Popular Playlists Featuring Can." I clicked on one playlist called "Irritation Mix," created by a user named Scotfree, whose avatar picture looks like Iron Man. The Can track included was the spacey instrumental "Spray," from the 1973 album *Future Days*. The rest of the playlist leaned on seventies rock—the Faces, Mott the Hoople, Iggy & the Stooges—but used recent tracks to keep things pleasantly unpredictable: Lady Sovereign's bubbly dance track "Blah Blah" and a track called "Johnny Depp," by the sixties revivalists Chocolat, from Montreal.

An album "collection" is no longer relevant for many listeners.

I didn't care for a few of the songs, but the experience was much more like grappling with a d.j. than like watching a piece of software operate. I learned about two bands I didn't know, was reminded of beloved tracks I had forgotten, and didn't listen to anything I already had in mind. Scotfree's playlist didn't last as long as a good d.j.'s shift; the burden is on the user to find other appealing users and more lists, and to build the experience. In some ways, it's an improvement on the radio model: the number of potentially appealing d.j.s here dwarfs what you might have once found on radio.

Music in a Cloud

The broadcast and on-demand models are governed by different rules, but they share one important feature: neither depends on downloading files or finding storage space on a personal computer. Lurking behind these models are two enormous companies that will likely change the landscape of online audio in a matter of months: Google and Apple. Google will soon offer a streaming music service for its Android phone that, like all of these services, uses the increasingly vital concept of the cloud—your music is all on a server, which you can access from any computer or smart phone, with little trouble and no wires. Apple, whose iTunes store is the biggest music retailer in America, bought the online streaming service Lala last year and then promptly shut it down. This suggests that there may soon be an iTunes.com, a Web-based streaming system that will leave behind the model of buying discrete tracks. In music's new model, fees are charged not necessarily so that you can physically possess a file but so that you can have that song whenever you want it.

An album "collection" is no longer relevant for many listeners. Limited only by the number of songs offered by any service—MOG offers nearly eight million—they can create as many playlists as they like, and access them from almost any device. Whoever comes up with the most powerful and elegant version of the streaming model will have a very big portal. If iTunes becomes a dominant radio force, it could control an overwhelming portion of the music business. Google owns YouTube, which already serves as a sort of ad-hoc radio station for many young people. If Google's streaming service works well with its Android applications and creates a music-bundling system, it, too, could take over a large share of the market.

While using these services, I kept thinking about an early-eighties drum machine called the Roland TR-808, which has seduced generations of musicians with its heavy kick-drum sound and the oddly human swing of its clock. Whoever programmed this box had more impact on dance music than the hundreds of better-known musicians who used the device. Similarly, the anonymous programmers who write the algorithms that control the series of songs in these streaming services may end up having a huge effect on the way that people think of musical narrative—what follows what, and who sounds best with whom. Sometimes we will be the d.j.s, and sometimes the machines will be, and we may be surprised by which we prefer.

Organizations to Contact

The editors have compiled the following list of organizations concerned with the issues debated in this book. The descriptions are derived from materials provided by the organizations. All have publications or information available for interested readers. The list was compiled on the date of publication of the present volume; names, addresses, phone and fax numbers, and e-mail and Internet addresses may change. Be aware that many organizations take several weeks or longer to respond to inquiries, so allow as much time as possible.

American Federation of Musicians of the United States and Canada (AFM)
1501 Broadway, Suite 600, New York, NY   10036
(212) 869-1330 • fax: (212) 764-6134
e-mail: presoffice@afm.org
website: www.afm.org

AFM is the largest organization in the world representing the interests of professional musicians. The organization negotiates fair agreements, protects ownership of recorded music, secures benefits such as health care and pensions, and lobbies legislators. The AFM website includes information, such as current news stories relevant to musicians, for the general public, as well as resources for members-only. The group also publishes the magazine *International Musician*.

American Society of Composers, Authors and Publishers (ASCAP)
1 Lincoln Plaza, New York, NY   10023
(212) 621-6000 • fax: (212) 724-9064
e-mail: info@ascap.com
website: www.ascap.com

ASCAP is a membership association of more than 330,000 US composers, songwriters, lyricists, and music publishers. AS-CAP protects the rights of its members by licensing and distributing royalties for the non-dramatic public performances of their copyrighted works. ASCAP publishes *The ASCAP Advantage* and provides information about its other activities on its website.

Electronic Frontier Foundation (EFF)

454 Shotwell St., San Francisco, CA 94110-1914
(415) 436-9333 • fax: (415) 436-9993
e-mail: information@eff.org
website: www.eff.org

The Electronic Frontier Foundation (EFF) is a grassroots legal advocacy nonprofit supported by member contributions. The organization specializes in cases in which it can help shape law in the areas of digital freedom, including more consumer-friendly file sharing rules. Its website offers a blog with the latest news of "the electronic frontier."

Future of Music Coalition (FMC)

1615 L St. NW, Suite 520, Washington, DC 20036
(202) 822-2051
e-mail: summit@futureofmusic.org
website: www.futureofmusic.org

The Future of Music Coalition (FMC) is a nonprofit collaboration between members of the music, technology, public policy, and intellectual property law communities that seeks to bring together diverse voices to identify and find creative solutions to the new challenges of technology. FMC publishes *The FMC Newsletter*.

Just Plain Folks Music Organization

5327 Kit Dr., Indianapolis, IN 46237
e-mail: justplainfolks@aol.com
website: www.jpfolks.com

Just Plain Folks Music Organization is a networking group for people in the music industry, including musicians, journalists, and retailers. The organization facilitates online networking as well as face-to-face meetings. Its website offers a member database, blog, resources, and news about the music industry.

National Music Publishers' Association (NMPA)
101 Constitution Ave. NW, Suite 705 E
Washington, DC   20001
(202) 742-4375 • fax: (202) 742-4377
e-mail: pr@nmpa.org
website: www.nmpa.org

The National Music Publishers' Association (NMPA) is the largest US music publishing trade association. NMPA represents its members to protect their property rights on the legislative, litigation, and regulatory fronts. NMPA publishes the newsletter *NMPA News and Views.*

The Recording Academy
3402 Pico Blvd., Santa Monica, CA   90405
(310) 392-3777 • fax: (310) 399-3090
e-mail: memservices@grammy.com
website: www.grammy.org/recording-academy

The Recording Academy's mission is "to positively impact the lives of musicians, industry members and our society at large." The group's work focuses on advocacy, music education, and philanthropy. The Recording Academy is also known for presenting the Grammy Awards, the most prestigious music award given in the United States. The group also publishes *Grammy Magazine.*

Recording Industry Association of America (RIAA)
1025 F St. NW, 10th Floor, Washington, DC   20004
(202) 775-0101
website: www.riaa.com

RIAA is the trade group that represents the US recording industry. The organization protects the intellectual property rights of artists and is the official certification agency for gold, platinum, and multi-platinum sales awards. RIAA publishes the newsletter *Fast Tracks*, which is available on its website, along with other news and blogs related to the recording industry.

Songwriters Guild of America (SGA)

5120 Virginia Way, Suite C22, Brentwood, TN   37027
(615) 742-9945 • fax: (615) 742-9948
e-mail: nash@songwritersguild.com
website: www.songwritersguild.com

SGA is a songwriters association that advocates on issues of importance to songwriters and the music industry in general, including home taping, derivative rights, author's moral rights, and, most recently, infringement of royalty payment due to digital/Internet piracy. SGA publishes the newsletter *Songwriters Guild of America* and provides other information and resources to SGA members on its website.

Bibliography

Books

Bob Baker	*Guerrilla Music Marketing Online: 129 Free & Low-Cost Strategies to Promote and Sell Your Music on the Internet.* St. Louis, MO: Spotlight, 2012.
Dean Budnick and Josh Baron	*Ticket Masters: The Rise of the Concert Industry and How the Public Got Scalped.* Toronto: ECW Press, 2011.
Steve Knopper	*Appetite for Self-Destruction: The Spectacular Crash of the Record Industry in the Digital Age.* New York: Soft Skull, 2009.
Greg Kot	*Ripped: How the Wired Generation Revolutionized Music.* New York: Scribner, 2010.
David Kusek and Gerd Leonhard	*The Future of Music: Manifesto for the Digital Music Revolution.* Boston: Berklee Press, 2005.
Lawrence Lessig	*Free Culture: The Nature and Future of Creativity.* New York: Penguin, 2005.
Lawrence Lessig	*Remix: Making Art and Commerce Thrive in the Hybrid Economy.* New York: Penguin, 2008.

Robert Levine — *Free Ride: How Digital Parasites Are Destroying the Culture Business, and How the Culture Business Can Fight Back.* New York: Doubleday, 2011.

Craig Marks and Rob Tannenbaum — *I Want My MTV: The Uncensored Story of the Music Video Revolution.* New York: Dutton Adult, 2011.

Kembrew McLeod and Lawrence Lessig — *Freedom of Expression: Resistance and Repression in the Age of Intellectual Property.* Minneapolis: University of Minnesota Press, 2007.

Michael Miller — *The Ultimate Digital Music Guide: The Best Way to Store, Organize, and Play Digital Music.* Indianapolis: Que, 2012.

William Patry — *How to Fix Copyright.* New York: Oxford University Press, 2012.

William Patry — *Moral Panics and the Copyright Wars.* New York: Oxford University Press, 2009.

Jonathan Zittrain — *The Future of the Internet—And How to Stop It.* New Haven, CT: Yale University Press, 2009.

Periodicals and Internet Sources

Andrew Baker — "Royalties Revamped for Digital," *Daily Variety*, April 12, 2012.

Christopher Breen — "Field of Streams: With Five Major Streaming Music Services, How Do You Pick the Right One?" *Macworld*, September 2012.

Christopher Breen "First Look: Amazon Cloud Player App," *Macworld*, September 2012.

Antony Bruno "Cloud Shapes: Artists and Fans See Different Things in Cloud Services," *Billboard*, May 14, 2011.

Ed Christman "The Future Is Unwritten: Are Catalog Moves Killing or Saving the CD?" *Billboard*, July 7, 2012.

Economist "Universal's Gamble: The Music Business," July 21, 2012.

Financial Express "Back Up Your Digital Life," August 9, 2012.

Financial Express "Listen to Music on the Go," August 2, 2012.

Jason Maderer and Liz Klipp "Music Robot Companion Enhances Listener Experience," *Space Daily*, July 23, 2012.

Marketing Week "Waxing Lyrical About the Future of Music Discovery," May 24, 2012.

PC Magazine "Amazon Cloud Player Comes to Sonos Wireless HiFi System," August 9, 2012. www.pcmag.com.

PC Magazine "Independent Musicians and Their Fans Gain Music Service," August 15, 2011. www.pcmag.com.

Glenn Peoples "Swelling Stream: What's the Potential Value of the Streaming Music Market?" *Billboard*, September 24, 2011.

Ben Shepherd	"Music Content Makers Take Total Control," *Encore Magazine*, June 2012.
Ray Waddell	"The Raw Deal," *Billboard*, March 10, 2012.

Index

M

N